# cool & fresh

leafy salads • pasta salads • seafood salads
meat salads

mc
rae
PUBLISHING

mc rae
PUBLISHING

This book was conceived,
edited and designed by
McRae Publishing Ltd
London

www.mcraepublishing.co.uk

**NOTE TO OUR READERS**
Eating eggs or egg whites that are not completely cooked poses the possibility of
salmonella food poisoning. The risk is greater for pregnant women, the elderly, the very
young, and persons with impaired immune systems. If you are concerned about
salmonella, you can use reconstituted powdered egg whites or pasteurized eggs.

*Culinary Notebooks series*

Project Director  Anne McRae
Art Director  Marco Nardi

COOL & FRESH
Photography  Brent Parker Jones
Text  Carla Bardi
Editing  Foreign Concept
Food Styling  Lee Blaylock
Food Styling Assistant  Rochelle Seator
Prop Styling  Lee Blaylock
Layouts  Filippo Delle Monache

ISBN 978-88-6098-331-2

Printed in China

# contents

# getting started

There are more than 100 delicious recipes for salads in this book. Almost all of them are simple and require only basic skills and a few minutes to prepare. All recipes have been rated for difficulty: 1 (simple) or 2 (fairly simple). In these pages we have chosen 25 of the most enticing recipes, just to get you started!

SICILIAN ORANGE salad

PECORINO WITH
PEARS & manuka honey

A HANDFUL
of green leaves

NEW POTATO
salad

SHRIMP COCKTAIL
with mango

BELL PEPPER, BEAN
& ARTICHOKE salad

BROWN RICE SALAD
with apples & walnuts

SEAFOOD
salad

CHICKEN & FRUIT
salad

BARLEY SALAD with tuna & mozzarella

PINZIMONIO (Tuscan raw veggie salad)

GREEK salad

REMOULADE

NIÇOISE salad

FATTOUSH
(Levantine bread salad)

CARIBBEAN salad

FARRO SALAD with apples,
gorgonzola & honey

BBQ PORK SALAD with fresh fruit

PANZANELLA
(Tuscan bread salad)

WARM THAI CHICKEN
salad

BEST LEAFY SALAD

ARUGULA with red apple,
walnuts & parmesan

BEST PASTA SALAD

PASTA SALAD with
roasted bell peppers

BEST RICE SALAD

WILD RICE SALAD
with dried fruit

BEST SEAFOOD SALAD

WARM & SPICY
fish salad

BEST MEAT SALAD

CHICKEN, BEAN
& ARUGULA salad

## CARIBBEAN salad

1 large orange, peeled and cut into segments

2 slices fresh pineapple, peeled, cored, and cut into cubes

Flesh from 1 coconut, cut into cubes

12 cherry tomatoes, quartered

1 yellow bell pepper (capsicum), seeded and thinly sliced

$^1/_4$ cup (60 ml) extra-virgin olive oil

1 tablespoon wholegrain mustard

Salt and freshly ground black pepper

1 small head romain (cos) lettuce

2 bananas, sliced

Freshly squeezed juice of 1 lime

Serves 2-4 • Preparation 15 minutes • Difficulty 1

1. Combine the orange, pineapple, and coconut in a large bowl. Add the tomatoes and bell pepper and mix well.

2. Whisk the oil and mustard in a small bowl. Season with salt and pepper.

3. Line a large salad bowl with the lettuce leaves. Spoon the salad ingredients on top of the lettuce and drizzle with the oil and mustard mixture.

4. Arrange the bananas on top. Drizzle with the lime juice. Serve at once.

If you liked this recipe, you will love these as well.

**PINEAPPLE** salad

**SICILIAN ORANGE** salad

**STRAWBERRY & FENNEL** salad

Manuka honey is harvested in New Zealand from bees that feed on the flowers of the wild manuka bush. It is believed to have antibacterial properties that help to heal a variety of conditions, from sore throats and stomach aches to irritable bowel syndrome. It is exported all over the world, but you can replace it with another local honey if preferred.

# PECORINO WITH PEARS & manuka honey

| | |
|---|---|
| 2-4 | tasty ripe eating pears, preferably organic |
| 2 | tablespoons freshly squeezed lemon juice |
| 4-5 | tablespoons manuka honey |
| 8 | ounces (250 g) pecorino cheese (young or aged, as preferred) |

Serves 4 • Preparation 10 minutes • Difficulty 1

1. If using organic pears, leave the peel on—they make the dish so much tastier.

2. Core the pears and cut into wedges. Drizzle with the lemon juice to stop them from turning brown. Drizzle with the honey,

3. Slice the cheese thinly and arrange the pears and cheese on a serving dish. Serve at once.

If you liked this recipe, you will love these as well.

**BABY SPINACH** with grapefruit & parmesan

**ARUGULA** with red apple, walnuts & parmesan

**CHEESE, PEAR & KIWI FRUIT** salad

# A HANDFUL of green leaves

Serves 6 • Preparation 10 minutes • Difficulty 1

**Salad**

| | |
|---|---|
| 1/2 | head frisée (curly endive) |
| 1/2 | head crisp romaine (cos) lettuce |
| 1 | cup (50 g) baby spinach |
| | Handful of arugula (rocket) |
| | Handful of watercress, tough stems discarded |
| | Handful of red radicchio or chard |
| 2 | tablespoons flat-leaf parsley leaves |

**Dressing**

| | |
|---|---|
| 1/4 | cup (60 ml) extra-virgin olive oil |
| 2 | tablespoons balsamic vinegar |
| | Salt and freshly ground black pepper |

**Salad**

1. Separate the leaves of the endive and romaine lettuce, discarding the bitter outer leaves. Tear into manageable pieces. Combine all the greens in a bowl and toss well.

**Dressing**

1. Whisk the oil, vinegar, salt, and pepper in a small bowl. Drizzle over the salad and toss well. Serve immediately.

# CRUDITIÉS with saffron dip

Serves 6 • Preparation 15 minutes + 20 minutes to rest
Cooking 3–5 minutes  Difficulty 1

| | | | |
|---|---|---|---|
| 4 | scallions (spring onions) | 2 | tablespoons freshly squeezed lemon juice |
| 1 | small cauliflower | 1 | tablespoon horseradish |
| 4 | stalks celery | | Salt and freshly ground black pepper |
| 4 | zucchini (courgettes) | | |
| 12 | radishes | 1/3 | cup (90 ml) extra-virgin olive oil |
| 2 | small red onions | | |
| 2 | heads red radicchio, torn | 1 | cup (250 g) fresh ricotta cheese, drained |
| | Pinch of saffron threads | 4 | tablespoons blanched pistachios, chopped |

1. Cut the scallions from the middle, sliding the knife toward the greener end. Repeat several times. Place in a bowl of iced water until the ends curl, 20 minutes.

2. Cook the cauliflower in salted boiling water until tender, 3–5 minutes. Drain and let cool. Slice the celery, zucchini, and radishes. Slice the onions into rings. Arrange on a serving dish with the radicchio.

3. Combine the saffron, lemon juice, and horseradish in a small bowl. Season with salt and pepper. Add the oil, ricotta, and pistachios and beat until well mixed. Put the bowl of dip on the serving dish and serve.

# Vegetarian SALADE NIÇOISE

Serves 4 • Preparation 30 minutes • Cooking 10–15 minutes
Difficulty 1

**Salad**

| | |
|---|---|
| 8 | ounces (250 g) baby potatoes |
| 8 | ounces (250 g) green beans, trimmed |
| 4 | boiled eggs, quartered |
| 3 | tomatoes, quartered |
| 3 | marinated artichokes, quartered |
| 1 | red onion, sliced |
| 1/4 | cup (25 g) small black olives |
| 1/4 | cup fresh parsley leaves |

**Dressing**

| | |
|---|---|
| 1/4 | cup (60 ml) extra-virgin olive oil |
| 2 | tablespoons freshly squeezed lemon juice |
| 1 | clove garlic, finely chopped |
| 1/2 | teaspoon Dijon mustard |
| | Salt and freshly ground black pepper |

**Salad**

1. Steam the potatoes until tender, 10–15 minutes. Cut in half. Blanch the beans until just tender, 2–3 minutes. Combine the eggs, potatoes, and green beans in a medium bowl and add the tomatoes, artichokes, onion, olives, and parsley.

**Dressing**

1. Whisk the oil, lemon juice, garlic, and mustard in a small bowl. Season with salt and pepper. Drizzle over the salad, toss to combine, and serve.

# PINEAPPLE salad

Serves 4 • Preparation 20 minutes • Cooking 5 minutes
Difficulty 1

**Salad**

| | | | |
|---|---|---|---|
| 8 | ounces (250 g) fresh or canned pineapple, drained, diced | 2 | scallions (spring onions), thinly sliced |
| 8 | ounces (250 g) bean sprouts | | **Dressing** |
| 1 | cup (100 g) toasted peanuts | 6 | tablespoons peanut butter |
| 2 | large carrots, grated | 2 | tablespoons vegetable oil |
| 1 | small cucumber, peeled and diced | 2 | teaspoons soy sauce |
| | | 1 | teaspoon white vinegar |
| | | 1 | teaspoon ground chile |
| | | 1/2 | cup (125 ml) cold water |

**Salad**

1. Combine the pineapple, bean sprouts, peanuts, carrots, cucumber, and scallions in a large salad bowl. Toss gently.

**Dressing**

1. Combine the peanut butter, oil, soy sauce, vinegar, and chile in a small saucepan over low heat. Stir, adding enough water to obtain a smooth, creamy dressing. Spoon over the salad, or serve separately in a small bowl so that guests can help themselves.

# BEET, ORANGE & FENNEL salad

### Salad

| | |
|---|---|
| 2 | teaspoons brown sugar |
| 2 | sprigs fresh rosemary, leaves removed and finely chopped |
| 3 | tablespoons extra-virgin olive oil |
| 1 | teaspoon salt |
| 4 | medium beets (beetroots), trimmed, with peel |
| 1 | bulb fennel, thinly sliced |
| 2 | oranges, peeled and broken into segments |

### Dressing

| | |
|---|---|
| 1 | small bunch fresh dill, finely chopped |
| 1/2 | cup (125 ml) extra-virgin olive oil |
| 2 | tablespoons balsamic vinegar |
| | Salt and freshly ground black pepper |
| 3/4 | cup (90 g) toasted hazelnuts |

Serves 4 • Preparation 15 minutes • Cooking 1 hour • Difficulty 1

## Salad

1. Preheat the oven to 350°F (180°C/gas 4). Mix the sugar, rosemary, oil, and salt in a small bowl. Add the beets and toss until well coated.

2. Wrap each beet in aluminum foil and place in a roasting pan. Roast until tender, about 1 hour. Peel and slice.

## Dressing

1. Whisk the dill, oil, and vinegar in a small bowl. Season with salt and pepper.

2. Arrange the beets on serving plates with the fennel and orange. Drizzle with the dressing, sprinkle with the nuts, and serve.

# SICILIAN ORANGE salad

4 oranges
1 small white onion, thinly sliced
1 tablespoon finely chopped fresh parsley
Salt and freshly ground black pepper
¹⁄₃ cup (90 ml) extra-virgin olive oil

Serves 4 • Preparation 10 minutes • Difficulty 1

1. Peel the oranges using a sharp knife, making sure that you remove all the white pith. Slice thinly.

2. Place the oranges in a large salad bowl. Add the onion and parsley and season with salt and pepper. Drizzle with the oil. Toss gently and serve.

This is a classic appetizer or side dish in Tuscany and also further south in Umbria. You will need the very best quality, cold pressed extra-virgin olive oil. Vary the vegetables according to the season and what you have on hand. If liked, whisk ½ cup (120 ml) of balsamic vinegar into the oil before dividing it among the little serving bowls.

**14**

# PINZIMONIO
## (Tuscan raw veggie salad)

| | |
|---|---|
| 4 | artichokes |
| | Freshly squeezed juice of 2 lemons |
| 4 | carrots (or 8 baby spring carrots) |
| 4 | celery hearts |
| 2 | large fennel bulbs |
| 12 | scallions (spring onions) |
| 12 | radishes |
| 1½ | cups (375 ml) extra-virgin olive oil |
| | Salt and freshly ground black pepper |

Serves 6 • Preparation 20 minutes • Difficulty 1

1. Remove all but the pale inner leaves from the artichokes by pulling the outer ones down and snapping them off. Cut off the stem and the top third of the remaining leaves. Cut in half lengthwise and scrape the fuzzy choke away with a knife. Cut in wedges and drizzle with the juice of 1 lemon

2. Scrub the carrots with a brush or peel and soak in a bowl of cold water with the remaining lemon juice for 10 minutes.

3. Discard the stringy outer stalks from the celery and trim off the leafy tops. Keep the inner white stalks and the heart.

4. Slice the bases off the fennel, trim away the leafy tops, and discard any blemished outer leaves. Cut into thin wedges.

5. Trim the scallions and radishes.

6. Whisk the oil with salt and pepper. Pour into six small bowls, so that each guest can dip their veggies into the oil as they eat.

If you liked this recipe, you will love these as well.

**CRUDITÉS**
with saffron dip

**RAW ENERGY**
salad

**PANZANELLA**
(Tuscan bread salad)

# ASIAN coleslaw

### Salad

| | |
|---|---|
| 1/2 | Chinese cabbage (wom bok), finely shredded |
| 2 | carrots, julienned |
| 2 | cups (120 g) snow pea shoots |
| 1/2 | cup (80 g) peanuts, toasted and chopped |
| 1 | red bell pepper (capsicum), julienned |
| 5 | scallions (spring onions), thinly sliced |
| 1/4 | cup (25 g) finely chopped fresh mint |
| 1/4 | cup (25 g) fresh cilantro (coriander) |

### Dressing

| | |
|---|---|
| 3 | tablespoons freshly squeezed lime juice |
| 1 1/2 | tablespoons Asian sesame oil |
| 1 | tablespoon soy sauce |
| 1 | clove garlic, minced |
| 1 | teaspoon finely grated fresh ginger |
| 1 | teaspoon finely grated jaggery (palm sugar) or brown sugar |
| | Salt and freshly ground black pepper |

Serves 4 • Preparation 15 minutes • Difficulty 1

### Salad

1. Combine the cabbage, carrots, snow pea shoots, peanuts, bell pepper, scallions, mint, and cilantro in a large bowl.

### Dressing

2. Whisk the lime juice, sesame oil, soy sauce, garlic, ginger, and palm sugar in a small bowl. Pour over the salad and toss to combine. Season with salt and pepper and serve.

# RAW ENERGY salad

## Salad

¼ cup (45 g) pumpkin seeds

¼ cup (45 g) sunflower seeds

2 tablespoons sesame seeds

2 teaspoons cumin seeds

¼ red cabbage, finely shredded

1 large carrot, grated

1 cooked beet (beetroot), grated

2 cups (100 g) baby spinach leaves, finely chopped

1 red onion, thinly sliced

¼ cup (45 g) dried currants

3 tablespoons finely chopped fresh mint

## Dressing

Finely grated zest and juice of 1 organic orange

3 tablespoons pomegranate molasses

1 tablespoon extra-virgin olive oil

Salt and freshly ground black pepper

## Salad

1. Toast the pumpkin, sunflower, sesame, and cumin seeds in a medium frying pan over medium heat until golden brown, 3-5 minutes.

2. Combine the red cabbage, carrot, beet, spinach, onion, currants, mint, and toasted seeds in a large salad bowl.

## Dressing

1. Whisk the orange zest and juice, pomegranate molasses, and oil in a small bowl. Pour over the salad and toss to combine. Season with salt and pepper and serve.

This light salad is packed with vitamins and goodness. Serve it as a starter before hearty pasta or meat dishes, or as a side dish with roast fish and meat. The grapefruit lightens the oil and fat in roast meats, cleansing the palette and enhancing the appetite.

# BABY SPINACH with grapefruit & parmesan

## Salad

| 4 | cups (200 g) baby spinach leaves |
|---|---|
| 4 | ounces (125 g) Parmesan cheese, in flakes |
| 1 | large grapefruit, cut into segments |

## Dressing

| | Freshly squeezed juice of $1/2$ lemon |
|---|---|
| 2 | tablespoons extra-virgin olive oil |
| 1 | tablespoon finely chopped fresh chives |
| | Salt and freshly ground black pepper |

Serves 4 • Preparation 10 minutes • Difficulty 1

## Salad

1. Arrange the spinach on four individual serving plates. Top with the Parmesan and grapefruit.

## Dressing

1. Whisk the lemon juice, oil, and chives in a small bowl. Season with salt and pepper.

2. Pour the dressing over the salad, toss well, and serve.

If you liked this recipe, you will love these as well.

CARIBBEAN salad

BEET, ORANGE & FENNEL salad

ORANGE & WATERCRESS salad

# MIXED TOMATO *salad*

## Salad

| | |
|---|---|
| 3 | plum tomatoes, sliced |
| 2 | green tomatoes, sliced |
| 12 | cherry tomatoes, halved |
| 6 | baby plum tomatoes, halved |
| | Salt and freshly ground black pepper |
| 1 | cup (50 g) arugula (rocket) |

## Dressing

| | |
|---|---|
| 8 | tablespoons (125 ml) extra-virgin olive oil |
| 1 | sweet onion, finely chopped |
| 2 | cloves garlic, minced |
| 2 | tablespoons coarsely chopped fresh parsley |
| 1 | teaspoon finely grated lemon zest |
| 5 | tablespoons freshly squeezed lemon juice |
| 1 | tablespoon red wine vinegar |
| 1/4 | cup (40 g) sundried tomatoes, drained |
| 2 | tablespoons coarsely torn fresh basil leaves |

Serves 4 • Preparation 20 minutes • Cooking 5 minutes • Difficulty 1

## Salad

1. Combine all the different types of tomatoes in a large bowl.

## Dressing

1. Heat 7 tablespoons (100 ml) of oil in a frying pan over low heat. Add the onion, garlic, and parsley and sauté until tender, 3–4 minutes. Add the lemon zest, 4 tablespoons lemon juice, vinegar, and sundried tomatoes and simmer until warm. Remove from the heat and add the basil leaves.

2. Season the tomatoes lightly with salt and pepper, spoon the warm dressing over the top, and toss gently.

3. Put the arugula in a small bowl and drizzle with the remaining oil and lemon juice. Mix the arugula into the tomatoes and serve.

# STRAWBERRY & FENNEL *salad*

**Salad**

| | |
|---|---|
| $^2/_3$ | cup (100 g) blanched almonds |
| 7 | cups (350 g) baby spinach leaves |
| 2 | cups (300 g) strawberries, sliced |
| 1 | fennel bulb, thinly sliced |

**Dressing**

| | |
|---|---|
| | Freshly squeezed juice of $^1/_2$ lemon |
| | Freshly squeezed juice of 1 orange |
| $^1/_3$ | cup (90 ml) extra-virgin olive oil |
| 2 | tablespoons balsamic vinegar |
| 1 | teaspoon Dijon mustard |
| | Salt and freshly ground black pepper |

Serves 4 • Preparation 10 minutes • Cooking 5 minutes • Difficulty 1

## Salad

1. Toast the almonds in a large frying pan over medium heat until golden brown, about 5 minutes. Remove from the heat and let cool.

2. Combine the spinach, strawberries, fennel, and almonds in a large salad bowl. Toss gently.

## Dressing

1. Whisk the lemon juice, orange juice, oil, vinegar, and mustard in a small bowl with a fork. Season with salt and pepper.

2. Drizzle the dressing over the salad, toss gently, and serve.

21

If melon is out of season or unavailable, replace with fresh or well drained canned pineapple.

# MELON, ZUCCHINI & PANCETTA salad

5      ounces (150 g) pancetta
       or bacon, diced

2      zucchini (courgettes),
       very thinly sliced

       Freshly squeezed juice
       of ¹/₂ lemon

1      cantaloupe (rock) melon,
       peeled, seeded, and cut into
       cubes

8      ounces (250 g) honeydew
       melon, peeled, seeded, and
       cut into cubes

1      cup (50 g) curly endive
       (frisée), coarsely shredded

       Salt and freshly ground black
       pepper

¹/₄    cup (60 ml) extra-virgin
       olive oil

       Fresh mint leaves, to garnish

Serves 4 • Preparation 15 minutes + 10 minutes to rest • Cooking 3-4 minutes • Difficulty 1

1. Sauté the pancetta in a small frying pan over medium heat until it starts to brown, 3-4 minutes. Remove from the heat and set aside.

2. Arrange the slices of zucchini on a large plate. Drizzle with the lemon juice and let rest for 10 minutes.

3. Put the melon in a large salad bowl with the zucchini, pancetta, and endive. Toss gently.

4. Arrange the salad in four serving dishes. Season with salt and pepper and drizzle with the oil. Garnish with the mint and serve.

If you liked this recipe, you will love these as well.

**WILD RICE SALAD**
with dried fruit

**CHICKEN & FRUIT**
salad

**BBQ PORK SALAD**
with fresh fruit

# APPLE SALAD with yogurt

$^1/_3$  cup (90 ml) plain yogurt
$^1/_3$  cup (90 ml) mayonnaise
1  tablespoon Dijon mustard
1  tablespoon cider vinegar
1  head romaine lettuce, coarsely shredded
1  organic red apple, cored and cut into thin wedges
1  organic green apple, cored and cut into thin wedges
1  small head celery, sliced
$^1/_2$  cup (80 g) walnuts, coarsely chopped
   Salt and freshly ground black pepper

Serves 4 • Preparation 10 minutes • Difficulty 1

1. Whisk the yogurt, mayonnaise, mustard, and vinegar in a small bowl.

2. Arrange the lettuce in a large salad bowl. Add the apples, celery, and walnuts. Drizzle with the dressing and season with salt and pepper. Toss gently and serve.

# ARUGULA WITH RED APPLE,
## walnuts & parmesan

4 cups (200 g) arugula (rocket)

4 ounces (125 g) Parmesan cheese, in flakes

1 large organic Red Delicious apple

Freshly squeezed juice of $1/2$ lemon

16 walnuts, coarsely chopped

$1/4$ cup (60 ml) extra-virgin olive oil

2 tablespoons white wine vinegar

1 teaspoon Dijon mustard

Salt and freshly ground black pepper

Serves 4 • Preparation 15 minutes • Difficulty 1

1. Place the arugula a in a large salad bowl. Top with the Parmesan.

2. Cut the apple in half, remove the core, and cut into small dice. Drizzle with the lemon juice and add to the salad. Sprinkle with the walnuts.

3. Whisk the oil, vinegar, and mustard in a small bowl. Season with salt and pepper.

4. Drizzle the dressing over the salad. Toss gently and serve.

Serve this pretty salad as an appetizer or pack it in plastic containers for a picnic spread. The colorful vegetables, seeds, and fruit will not only delight your guests but will also nurture them since they are packed with vitamins and antioxidants.

# ORANGE & WATERCRESS salad

Serves 4 • Preparation 15 minutes • Cooking 1–2 minutes • Difficulty 1

## Salad

| | |
|---|---|
| 2 | cups (100 g) watercress |
| 2 | large organic oranges |
| 3 | carrots, grated |
| 1 | head green or red radicchio, torn |
| 1 | fresh pomegranate |
| 1 | tablespoon sunflower seeds |
| 1 | tablespoon pumpkin seeds |

## Dressing

| | |
|---|---|
| 2 | tablespoons freshly squeezed lemon juice |
| 1 | teaspoon Dijon mustard |
| 1/4 | cup (60 ml) grapeseed oil or sunflower oil |
| | Salt and freshly ground black pepper |

## Salad

1. Put the watercress in a salad bowl. Grate the orange zest and set aside for the dressing. Peel the oranges and pare off the white pith. Cut the flesh crosswise into thin slices, removing any seeds, and add to the bowl. Add the carrots and radicchio.

2. Open the pomegranate, cut into sections, and remove the seeds. Add the seeds to the bowl.

3. Toast the sunflower and pumpkin seeds in a pan over high heat until nutty, 1–2 minutes.

## Dressing

1. Whisk the lemon juice, mustard, reserved orange zest, and oil in a small bowl. Season with salt and pepper.

2. Drizzle over the salad and toss. Garnish with the toasted seeds and serve.

If you liked this recipe, you will love these as well.

**KIWI, MUSHROOM & HAZELNUT** salad

**FATTOUSH** (Levantine bread salad)

**SHRIMP COCKTAIL** with mango

This is a traditional Sicilian recipe. You can make a lighter version by grilling the eggplant instead of frying it.

# SPICY EGGPLANT salad

| | |
|---|---|
| 1 | large eggplant (aubergine), with skin, cut into small cubes |
| 1 | tablespoon coarse sea sat |
| 1 | cup (250 ml) olive oil, for frying |
| 1 | small green bell pepper (capsicum), seeded, cored, and cut into small cubes |
| 1 | small yellow bell pepper (capsicum), seeded, cored, and cut into small cubes |
| 6 | radishes, cut into small cubes |
| 4 | scallions (spring onions), finely chopped |
| 2 | tomatoes, and cut into small cubes |
| 2 | cloves garlic, finely chopped |
| 3 | tablespoons finely chopped fresh parsley |
| 1 | teaspoon cumin seeds |
| 1 | teaspoon red pepper flakes |
| $\frac{1}{2}$ | teaspoon salt |
| $\frac{1}{4}$ | cup (60 ml) freshly squeezed lime juice |

Serves 4 • Preparation 15 minutes + 1 hour to drain • Cooking 20 minutes • Difficulty 1

1. Place the eggplant in a colander. Sprinkle with the coarse sea salt and let drain for 1 hour.

2. Heat the oil in a large frying pan. Fry the eggplant in batches until tender, 5–7 minutes. Drain well on paper towels and let cool.

3. Transfer the eggplant to a large bowl. Mix in the bell peppers, radishes, scallions, tomatoes, garlic, parsley, cumin, red pepper flakes, salt, and lime juice. Toss gently and serve.

If you liked this recipe, you will love these as well.

**PASTA SALAD** with grilled summer veggies

**PASTA SALAD** with eggplant & pine nuts

**COUSCOUS SALAD** with eggplant

# WARM BUTTER BEAN salad

8   ounces (250 g) dried butter
    beans or lima beans
3   cloves garlic, finely chopped
1/2 teaspoon red pepper flakes
2   tablespoons extra-virgin
    olive oil
4   ounces (120 g) prosciutto,
    coarsely chopped
    Salt and freshly ground black
    pepper
    Fresh basil leaves, to garnish
1   cup (50 g) arugula (rocket)

Serves 4 • Preparation 20 minutes + 12 hours to soak • Cooking 1 hour
Difficulty 2

1. Soak the butter beans in a large bowl of warm water
   overnight. Drain and place in a large pot of cold water.
   Bring to a boil. Cover and simmer until just tender, about
   1 hour. Drain, reserving 1 cup (250 ml) of the cooking water.

2. Sauté the garlic and red pepper flakes in the oil in a
   medium saucepan over medium heat until the garlic turns
   pale gold, 2-3 minutes. Add the prosciutto and sauté over
   medium heat until crisp, about 2 minutes.

3. Add the butter beans and cook, stirring occasionally, until
   heated through. Add some of the reserved cooking water
   if the mixture seems a little dry. Season with salt and
   pepper and add the torn basil leaves and arugula.
   Toss gently and serve warm.

# BELL PEPPER, BEAN & ARTICHOKE salad

2    red bell peppers (capsicums)

8    ounces (250 g) green beans, cut into short lengths

8    ounces (250 g) canned butter beans or lima beans, drained

14   ounces (400 g) canned artichoke hearts, drained and cut in half

$^1/_4$   cup (60 ml) extra-virgin olive oil

2    tablespoons white wine vinegar

Salt and freshly ground black pepper

Fresh basil leaves, to garnish

Serves 4 • Preparation 30 minutes • Cooking 15–20 minutes • Difficulty 1

1. Preheat an overhead broiler (grill) to hot. Place the bell peppers underneath and cook until blackened all over, turning often, about 15 minutes. Place in a plastic bag and set aside for 10 minutes. Pick off all the blackened skin and remove the seeds. Wipe clean with kitchen paper and chop into long thin strips.

2. Cook the green beans in a pot of salted boiling water until just tender, 5–7 minutes. Drain and let cool under cold running water. Set aside.

3. Mix the green beans, bell peppers, butter beans, artichoke hearts, oil, and vinegar in a large bowl. Season with salt and pepper. Toss well. Garnish with the basil and serve.

Serve this salad as an appetizer or as a lunch dish together with some fresh, light cheese.

# KIWI, MUSHROOM & HAZELNUT salad

$^1/_2$ cup (80 g) hazelnuts

4 slices bread, crusts removed and cut into cubes

1 clove garlic, lightly crushed but whole

4 tablespoons (60 ml) extra-virgin olive oil

5 cups (250 g) mixed salad greens

12 button mushrooms, thinly sliced

Salt and freshly ground black pepper

5 ounces (150 g) Parmesan cheese, cut into flakes

2 ripe kiwi fruit, peeled and thinly sliced

Serves 4 • Preparation 20 minutes • Cooking 10 minutes • Difficulty 1

1. Preheat the oven to 400°F (200°C/gas 6). Spread the hazelnuts out on a baking sheet and toast for 5 minutes, until lightly browned. Let cool slightly.

2. Sauté the bread with the garlic in 2 tablespoons of oil in a small frying pan over medium heat until crisp and golden brown, about 5 minutes. Drain well on paper towels. Discard the garlic.

3. Combine the salad greens and mushrooms in a large bowl. Drizzle with the remaining 2 tablespoons of oil and season with salt and pepper.

4. Divide the salad among four serving dishes. Top with the Parmesan, kiwi fruit, hazelnuts, and croutons and serve.

If you liked this recipe, you will love these as well.

**APPLE SALAD**
with yogurt

**CHEESE, PEAR & KIWI FRUIT** salad

**BROWN RICE SALAD**
with apples & walnuts

# GREEK SALAD with bell peppers & artichokes

### Salad

| | |
|---|---|
| 2 | red bell peppers (capsicums) |
| 3/4 | cup (90 g) almonds |
| 3 | cups (150 g) baby spinach |
| 5 | ounces (150 g) feta cheese, cut into cubes |
| 8 | ounces (250 g) canned artichoke hearts, quartered |
| 1/2 | cup (50 g) black olives, pitted |
| | Pita bread, to serve |

### Dressing

| | |
|---|---|
| 1/2 | cup (125 ml) extra-virgin olive oil |
| 1/4 | cup (60 ml) freshly squeezed lemon juice |
| 2 | teaspoons honey |
| 2 | teaspoons finely chopped fresh oregano |
| | Salt and freshly ground black pepper |

Serves 4–6 • Preparation 15 minutes + 10 minutes to rest • Cooking 15 minutes • Difficulty 2

## Salad

1. Preheat an overhead broiler (grill) to hot. Place the bell peppers underneath and cook until blackened all over, turning often. Place in a plastic bag and set aside for 10 minutes. Pick off all the blackened skin and remove the seeds. Wipe clean with kitchen paper. Slice into thin strips.

2. Toast the almonds in a small frying pan over medium-high heat until crisp and golden, 2–3 minutes.

3. Mix the bell pepper, almonds, spinach, feta, artichoke hearts, and olives in a large salad bowl.

## Dressing

1. Whisk the oil, lemon juice, honey, and oregano in a small bowl until well combined. Season with salt and pepper.

2. Drizzle the dressing over the salad and toss well. Serve with the pita bread.

# GREEK salad

2 cucumbers, thinly sliced

4 firm-ripe tomatoes, coarsely chopped

2 red onions, sliced

5 ounces (150 g) feta cheese, crumbled

$^{1}/_{2}$ cup (50 g) kalamata olives

5 tablespoons (75 ml) extra-virgin olive oil

2 tablespoons balsamic vinegar

Salt and freshly ground black pepper

Fresh oregano leaves, to garnish

Serves 4 • Preparation 10 minutes • Difficulty 1

1. Combine the cucumbers, tomatoes, onions, feta, and olives in a salad bowl.

2. Whisk the oil and vinegar in a small bowl until well blended.

3. Drizzle the dressing over the salad. Season with salt and pepper. Toss gently, garnish with the oregano, and serve.

Like many of the salads in this book, this recipe is more of a starting point than a set list of ingredients to be followed scrupulously. If you don't like kiwi fruit or they are not available, replace them with another fruit, or leave them out while increasing the amount of pear. Feel free to experiment and follow your own tastes and inclinations. Preparing food should always be fun, not a chore.

# CHEESE, PEAR & KIWI FRUIT salad

| | |
|---|---|
| 3 | ripe kiwi fruit, peeled and cut into small cubes |
| 3 | large ripe pears, peeled, cored, and cut into cubes |
| 12 | ounces (350 g) Fontina, Edam, or other mild table cheese, cut into small cubes |
| 3 | cups (150 g) mixed salad greens, coarsely shredded |
| 1/4 | cup (50 g) golden raisins (sultanas) |
| 1/3 | cup (90 ml) extra-virgin olive oil |
| 3 | tablespoons balsamic vinegar |
| | Salt and freshly ground black pepper |

Serves 4 • Preparation 15 minutes • Difficulty 1

1. Combine the kiwi fruit, pears, Fontina, salad greens, and raisins in a large salad bowl.

2. Whisk the oil and vinegar in a small bowl. Season with salt and pepper.

3. Drizzle the dressing over the salad, toss well, and serve.

If you liked this recipe, you will love these as well.

**PECORINO WITH PEARS**
& manuka honey

**FARRO SALAD** with apples, gorgonzola & honey

**COUSCOUS SALAD**
with apple

# REMOULADE

Serves 6 • Preparation 20 minutes + 30 minutes to chill
Difficulty 2

| | | | |
|---|---|---|---|
| 1 | celery root (celeriac), weighing about 1 pound (500 g) | 1/4 | cup (60 ml) extra-virgin olive oil |
| 1 | small red onion, finely chopped | 1 | tablespoon single (light) cream |
| 1 | scallion (spring onion), finely chopped | 2 | tablespoons finely chopped fresh mint |
| 3 | tablespoons freshly squeezed lemon juice | | Salt and freshly ground black pepper |
| 2 | tablespoons mustard | | Arugula (rocket), to garnish |

1. Oil six 1-cup (250-ml) ramekins. Peel the celery root and grate coarsely. Mix the celery root, onion, scallion, and lemon juice in a large bowl.

2. Put the mustard in a small bowl. Gradually whisk in the oil until thick and creamy. Whisk in the cream and mint. Drizzle the dressing over the vegetables.

3. Season with salt and pepper. Spoon the vegetables into the prepared ramekins and chill for 30 minutes.

4. Turn out onto serving plates, garnish with arugula, and serve.

# LENTIL & HERB salad

Serves 6 • Preparation 20 minutes • Cooking 30–40 minutes • Difficulty 1

| | | | |
|---|---|---|---|
| 3/4 | cup (150 g) green lentils | 1/4 | cup (60 ml) extra-virgin olive oil + extra to drizzle |
| 1 | clove garlic, peeled | | |
| 1 | cup (50 g) watercress | 1 | tablespoon sherry or red wine vinegar |
| 3 | tablespoons finely chopped fresh parsley | | Salt and freshly ground black pepper |
| 3 | tablespoons finely chopped fresh basil | 1/2 | cup (60 g) pecorino cheese, shaved |
| 2 | tablespoons chopped fresh arugula (rocket) | 2 | lemons, to serve |

1. Rinse the lentils. Place in a saucepan, cover with cold water, and add the garlic. Bring to a boil, then simmer until tender, 30–40 minutes.

2. Chop half the watercress and add to a bowl with the parsley, basil, and rocket. Drain the lentils and remove the garlic. Stir in the oil and vinegar and season with salt and pepper. Add the herb mixture and toss well. Mix the remaining watercress leaves and pecorino into the salad.

3. Divide among six salad bowls. Drizzle with a little extra oil and serve with the lemon wedges.

# BEAN & ASPARAGUS salad

Serves 6 • Preparation 20 minutes • Cooking 5-10 minutes
Difficulty 1

**Salad**

| | | | |
|---|---|---|---|
| 8 | ounces (250 g) fresh fava (broad) beans | | cheese, cubed |
| 8 | ounces (250 g) green beans, trimmed | 5 | basil leaves, torn |
| | | | **Dressing** |
| 16 | asparagus stalks | 1/4 | cup (25 g) basil |
| 5 | ounces (150 g) snow peas (mangetout) | 2 | tablespoons white wine vinegar |
| 1 | (14-ounce/400-g) can kidney beans, drained | 1/3 | cup (90 ml) extra-virgin olive oil |
| 15 | black olives, pitted | 1 | clove garlic, peeled |
| 8 | ounces (250 g) feta | | Salt and freshly ground black pepper |

**Salad**

1. Cook the fava beans, green beans, and asparagus in salted boiling water for 3–4 minutes. Drain and let cool. Cook the snow peas in salted boiling water for 2 minutes. Drain and let cool.

**Dressing**

1. Chop the basil, vinegar, oil, garlic, salt, and pepper in a food processor.

2. Combine the vegetables, beans, olives, and cheese in a salad bowl. Drizzle with the dressing. Toss lightly. Sprinkle with the basil leaves and serve.

# ENDIVE & APRICOT salad

Serves 4 • Preparation 30 minutes + 2 hours to chill
Difficulty 2

| | | | |
|---|---|---|---|
| 3 | ounces (90 g) Gorgonzola cheese | 2 | teaspoons freshly squeezed lemon juice |
| 3 | ounces (90 g) cream cheese, softened | | Salt and freshly ground black pepper |
| 2 | heads Belgian endive | 1 | teaspoon Dijon mustard |
| 12 | button mushrooms, thinly sliced | 1 | tablespoon white wine vinegar |
| 4 | soaked dried apricots, finely chopped | 3 | tablespoons sour cream |
| | | | Fresh lemon juice |

1. Beat the Gorgonzola and cream cheese with a handheld blender until smooth.

2. Remove the endive leaves from their cores. Spread the inside of each leaf with cheese mixture, then sandwich back together into their original shape. Wrap in plastic wrap (cling film) and chill for 2 hours.

3. Combine the mushrooms and apricots in a small bowl. Drizzle with lemon juice. Season with salt and pepper.

4. Whisk the mustard, vinegar, sour cream, and a squeeze of lemon juice in a small bowl.

5. Unwrap the endives and cut into rounds. Top with the apricot mixture and dressing and serve.

# pasta & co.

## PASTA SALAD with roasted bell peppers

1    pound (500 g) farfalle or other short pasta

2    zucchini (courgettes), cut in small cubes

$1/2$    cup (125 ml) extra-virgin olive oil

1    large yellow bell pepper (capsicum)

1    large red bell pepper (capsicum)

5    ounces (150 g) feta cheese, crumbled

1    tablespoon salt-cured capers, rinsed

Zest of 1 lemon, yellow part only, cut in very small pieces

Salt

2    tablespoons coarsely chopped fresh basil + extra leaves, to garnish

Serves 4 • Preparation 20 minutes • Cooking 20–25 minutes
Difficulty 2

1. Cook the pasta in a large pot of salted boiling water until al dente. Add the zucchini to the pasta pan about 3 minutes before the pasta is cooked.

2. Drain well and run under cold running water. Drain again and dry on a clean kitchen towel. Place in a serving bowl with 2 tablespoons of oil. Toss gently to stop the pasta and zucchini from sticking together.

3. Broil (grill) the bell peppers under an overhead broiler (grill) until the skins are blackened. Place in a plastic bag, shut tight, and let rest for 10 minutes. Peel off the skins and cut in thin strips.

4. Add the bell peppers to the bowl along with the feta, capers, lemon zest, salt, basil, and remaining oil. Toss well. Garnish with the basil leaves and serve.

If you liked this recipe, you will love these as well.

**SPICY EGGPLANT** salad

**PASTA SALAD with** grilled summer veggies

**PASTA SALAD with** eggplant & pine nuts

# PASTA SALAD with yogurt & avocado

| | |
|---|---|
| 1 | pound (500 g) farfalle or other short pasta |
| 6 | tablespoons (90 ml) extra-virgin olive oil |
| 1 | large onion, chopped |
| 2 | cloves garlic, finely chopped |
| 1 | tablespoon dry white wine |
| 2 | ripe avocados, peeled, pitted, and diced |
| | Freshly squeezed juice of 1 lemon |
| 1 | cup (250 ml) plain yogurt |
| 1 | fresh red chile, thinly sliced |
| 1 | celery heart, thinly sliced |
| 2 | tablespoons salt-cured capers, rinsed |
| 3 | tablespoons finely chopped fresh parsley |
| | Salt and freshly ground black pepper |

Serves 4–6 • Preparation 15 minutes • Cooking 10–15 minutes
Difficulty 1

1. Cook the pasta in a large pot of salted boiling water until al dente. Drain well and let cool under cold running water. Drain again and dry on a clean kitchen towel. Place in a serving bowl with 2 tablespoons of oil. Toss gently.

2. Heat 2 tablespoons of oil in a frying pan over medium heat. Add the onion and garlic and sauté until softened, 3–4 minutes. Add the wine and cook until evaporated. Let cool.

3. Drizzle the avocados with the lemon juice to keep it from turning brown. Whisk the yogurt with the remaining 2 tablespoons of oil in a small bowl.

4. Add the avocado, onion mixture, chile, celery, capers, and parsley to the bowl with the pasta. Top with the yogurt mixture. Season with salt and pepper. Toss gently and serve.

# PASTA SALAD with tomatoes, feta & olives

1½ pounds (750 g) cherry tomatoes, quartered

1 small red onion, thinly sliced

1 clove garlic, finely chopped

8 ounces (250 g) feta cheese, cut into small cubes

⅓ cup (90 ml) extra-virgin olive oil

1 tablespoon finely chopped fresh basil + extra leaves, to garnish

1 tablespoon finely chopped fresh mint

Finely grated zest of 1 lemon

Salt and freshly ground black pepper

1 pound (500 g) penne or other short pasta

1 cup (100 g) black olives

Serves 4–6 • Preparation 15 minutes + 30 minutes to rest • Cooking 15 minutes • Difficulty 1

1. Combine the cherry tomatoes, onion, garlic, feta, oil, basil, mint, and lemon zest in a large salad bowl. Toss well and season with salt and pepper. Let rest for 30 minutes.

2. Cook the pasta in a large pot of salted boiling water until al dente. Drain well and let cool under cold running water. Drain again and dry on a clean kitchen towel.

3. Add the pasta to the bowl with the cherry tomato mixture. Add the olives and toss well. Garnish with basil and serve.

Add a clove of garlic to the tapenade mixture for extra flavor if liked. Black olive tapenade goes beautifully with pasta and is easy to prepare at home. However, if you are short of time, you can buy a can or bottle of ready-made tapenade for this recipe.

# PASTA SALAD with tapenade & veggies

44

| | |
|---|---|
| 1 | pound (500 g) spiral or other short pasta |
| 8 | ounces (250 g) green beans, trimmed |
| 2 | cups (200 g) large black olives, pitted |
| 1 | fresh red chile, seeded |
| 1 | bunch fresh parsley |
| $\frac{1}{3}$ | cup (90 ml) extra-virgin olive oil |
| 2 | cups (100 g) mixed baby salad greens |
| 16 | cherry tomatoes, halved |
| 1 | yellow bell pepper (capsicum), seeded and chopped |

Serves 4-6 • Preparation 15 minutes • Cooking 10-15 minutes
Difficulty 1

1. Cook the pasta in a large pan of salted boiling water. After it has been cooking for about 5 minutes, add the green beans and return to a boil as soon as possible. Cook until the pasta is al dente and the beans are just cooked, 5-7 more minutes. Drain well and let cool under cold running water. Drain again and dry on a clean kitchen towel.

2. Combine the olives, chile, parsley, and oil in a food processor and chop finely. Pour the olive sauce over the pasta and toss well.

3. Place the salad greens in the bottom of a large salad dish. Place the pasta on top of the salad greens and top with the cherry tomatoes and bell pepper. Serve.

If you liked this recipe, you will love these as well.

**BELL PEPPER, BEAN & ARTICHOKE** salad

**BEAN & ASPARAGUS** salad

**PASTA SALAD** with curry

# PASTA SALAD with cheese

Serves 4–6 • Preparation 15 minutes • Cooking 10–15 minutes • Difficulty 1

| | | | |
|---|---|---|---|
| 1 | pound (500 g) fusilli or other short pasta | 1 | fresh red chile, seeded and finely chopped |
| 1 | pound (500 g) cherry tomatoes, chopped | | Salt |
| 1/3 | cup (90 ml) extra-virgin olive oil | 5 | ounces (150 g) Emmental cheese, thinly sliced |
| 2 | tablespoons fresh basil leaves | 1 | cup (50 g) baby arugula (rocket) leaves |

1. Cook the pasta in a large pot of salted boiling water until al dente. Drain and rinse under cold running water. Drain again and dry on a clean kitchen towel.

2. Combine the cherry tomatoes, oil, basil, and chile in a large salad bowl. Season with salt.

3. Add the pasta to the bowl with the tomato mixture. Toss well. Top with the cheese and arugula, toss gently, and serve.

# PASTA SALAD with fresh tuna

Serves 4–6 • Preparation 15 minutes + 30 minutes to marinate • Cooking 10–15 minutes • Difficulty 2

| | | | |
|---|---|---|---|
| 14 | ounces (400 g) fresh tuna, skinned, boned, and chopped | | crushed but whole |
| | Freshly squeezed juice of 1 lemon | 1 | pound (500 g) tomatoes, chopped |
| 3/4 | cup (180 ml) extra-virgin olive oil | | Salt and freshly ground white pepper |
| 20 | black olives, pitted and chopped | 1 | pound (500 g) conchiglie or other short pasta |
| 2 | cloves garlic, lightly | 1 | tablespoon fresh basil |

1. Put the tuna in a bowl. Drizzle with the lemon juice and 1/4 cup (60 ml) of oil. Add the olives. Let marinate for 30 minutes.

2. Sauté the garlic in 1/4 cup (60 ml) of oil in a frying pan over medium heat for 1–2 minutes. Let cool. Discard the garlic. Mix the tomatoes and garlic-infused oil into the tuna. Season with salt and pepper.

3. Cook the pasta in a large pot of salted boiling water until al dente. Drain and let cool under running cold water. Drain again and dry on a clean kitchen towel. Transfer to a serving bowl. Drizzle with the remaining oil. Add the tuna sauce and basil. Toss well and serve.

# PASTA SALAD with curry

Serves 4–6 • Preparation 15 minutes + 1 hour to chill Cooking 10–15 minutes • Difficulty 1

| Salad | | Dressing | |
|---|---|---|---|
| 1 | pound (500 g) fusilli or other short pasta | 1/3 | cup (90 ml) extra-virgin olive oil |
| 1 | red bell pepper (capsicum), chopped | 2 | tablespoons white wine vinegar |
| 1 | green bell pepper (capsicum), chopped | 1/2 | teaspoon sugar |
| 4 | ounces (120 g) lean ham, cut into thin strips | 1 | teaspoon curry powder Salt and freshly ground black pepper |
| 2 | tablespoons snipped fresh chives | | |

### Salad

1. Cook the pasta in a large pot of salted boiling water until al dente. Drain and rinse under cold running water. Drain again and dry on a clean kitchen towel.

2. Put the pasta in a salad bowl with the bell peppers, ham, and chives. Toss well.

### Dressing

1. Whisk the oil, vinegar, sugar, and curry in a small bowl. Season with salt and pepper.

2. Drizzle the dressing over the salad and toss well. Chill in the refrigerator for 1 hour before serving.

# PASTA SALAD with ham

Serves 4–6 • Preparation 20 minutes • Cooking 10–15 minutes • Difficulty 1

| | | | |
|---|---|---|---|
| 1 | pound (500 g) farfalle (bow ties) or other short pasta | 2 | tablespoons freshly squeezed lemon juice |
| 3 | zucchini (courgettes), julienned | | Small bunch fresh basil |
| 2 | carrots, julienned | | Salt |
| 1/2 | cup (125 ml) extra-virgin olive oil | 1 | teaspoon freshly ground white pepper |
| 3 | tablespoons red wine vinegar | 8 | ounces (250 g) ham, diced |

1. Cook the pasta in a large pot of salted boiling water until al dente. About 3 minutes before the pasta is cooked, add the zucchini and carrots to the pot. Drain well and run under cold running water. Drain again and dry on a clean cloth.

2. Transfer to a serving bowl with 2 tablespoons of oil. Toss gently to stop the pasta and vegetables from sticking together.

3. Whisk the remaining oil, vinegar, lemon juice, basil, salt, and pepper in a small bowl.

4. Add the ham to the bowl with the pasta then drizzle with the oil mixture. Toss well and serve.

# PASTA SALAD with chicken & spinach

1    pound (500 g) penne or other short pasta
2    tablespoons butter
1    onion, finely chopped
1    clove garlic, finely chopped
2    cups (300 g) cooked chicken, shredded
½    cup (125 ml) chicken stock
2    cups (100 g) baby spinach leaves, coarsely chopped
     Salt and freshly ground black pepper
⅓    cup (60 g) pine nuts, toasted

Serves 4-6 • Preparation 15 minutes • Cooking 10-15 minutes
Difficulty 1

1. Cook the pasta in a large pot of salted, boiling water until al dente. Drain well and let cool under cold running water. Drain again and dry on a clean kitchen towel.

2. Heat the butter in a large frying pan over medium heat. Add the onion and garlic and sauté until softened, 3-4 minutes. Add the chicken and chicken stock. Simmer for 5 minutes then set aside to cool.

3. Put the pasta in a large salad bowl. Add the chicken mixture, spinach, and pine nuts. Season with salt and pepper. Toss well and serve.

# PASTA SALAD with grilled summer veggies

1   large eggplant (aubergine), with skin, thinly sliced

1   red bell pepper (capsicum), seeded and sliced

1   yellow bell pepper (capsicum), seeded and sliced

2   large zucchini (courgettes), thinly sliced

4   ripe tomatoes, sliced

8   ounces (250 g) mozzarella cheese, cut in small cubes

2   tablespoons finely chopped fresh basil

    Salt and freshly ground white pepper

6   tablespoons (90 ml) extra-virgin olive oil

1   pound (500 g) fusilli or other short pasta

Serves 4–6 • Preparation 30 minutes • Cooking 30 minutes • Difficulty 2

1. Preheat a grill pan over medium-high heat. Grill the eggplant, bell peppers, zucchini, and tomatoes until tender and marked with brown lines.

2. Put all the grilled vegetables in a large serving bowl with the mozzarella and sprinkle with the basil, salt, and pepper. Drizzle with the oil.

3. Cook the pasta in a large pot of salted, boiling water until al dente. Drain well and let cool under cold running water. Drain again and dry on a clean kitchen towel.

4. Add the pasta to the bowl with the vegetables, toss gently, and serve.

Canned tuna is very nutritious. It is a good source of protein, niacin, vitamins B6 and B12, selenium, and phosphorus. Choose a brand that is canned in water so that it will be low in fat.

# PASTA SALAD with tuna, cherry tomatoes & olives

| | |
|---|---|
| 8 | ounces (250 g) canned tuna, drained and crumbled |
| 1 | pound (500 g) cherry tomatoes, halved |
| 1 | cup (100 g) black olives, pitted and finely chopped |
| 2 | scallions (spring onions), coarsely chopped |
| 2 | stalks celery, coarsely chopped |
| 1 | carrot, coarsely chopped |
| 1 | clove garlic, finely chopped |
| 1/3 | cup (90 ml) extra-virgin olive oil |
| | Salt and freshly ground white pepper |
| 1 | teaspoon dried oregano |
| 1 | pound (500 g) conchiglie (shells) or other short pasta |
| 2 | tablespoons finely chopped fresh parsley |
| 2 | tablespoons fresh basil leaves |

Serves 4–6 • Preparation 20 minutes + 1 hour to chill • Cooking 10–15 minutes • Difficulty 1

1. Combine the tuna, tomatoes, olives, scallions, celery, carrot, and garlic in a bowl. Drizzle with the oil and season with salt, pepper, and oregano. Cover with plastic wrap (cling film) and refrigerate for 1 hour.

2. Cook the pasta in a large pot of salted boiling water until al dente. Drain well and let cool under cold running water. Drain again and dry on a clean kitchen towel.

3. Put the pasta in a serving bowl. Add the tuna mixture and toss well. Garnish with the parsley and basil and serve.

If you liked this recipe, you will love these as well.

46
PASTA SALAD
with fresh tuna

57
RICE SALAD
with tuna & avocado

62
BARLEY SALAD
with tuna & mozzarella

# PASTA SALAD with artichokes & parmesan

1     **pound (500 g) penne or other short pasta**

8     **small fresh artichokes**

       **Freshly squeezed juice of 1 lemon**

1/3   **cup (90 ml) extra-virgin olive oil**

5     **ounces (150 g) Parmesan cheese, in flakes**

       **Salt and freshly ground black pepper**

Serves 4-6 • Preparation 20 minutes • Cooking 10-15 minutes
Difficulty 2

1. Cook the pasta in a large pot of salted, boiling water until al dente. Drain well and let cool under cold running water. Drain again and dry on a clean kitchen towel.

2. Trim the artichoke stems, cut off the top third of each one, and remove the tough outer leaves by snapping them off. Cut in half lengthwise and scrape any fuzzy choke away with a knife. Slice thinly. Drizzle with the lemon juice and oil.

3. Put the pasta in a large salad bowl. Add the artichoke mixture and cheese. Season with salt and pepper. Toss well and serve.

# PASTA SALAD with eggplant & pine nuts

1 large eggplant (aubergine), with skin, thickly sliced

Coarse sea salt

1 cup (250 ml) olive oil, for frying

2 large yellow bell peppers (capsicums)

4 tablespoons (60 ml) extra-virgin olive oil

1 medium onion, finely chopped

2 cloves garlic, finely chopped

Salt

2 tablespoons pine nuts, toasted

1 pound (500 g) ridged ditalini or other short pasta

2 tablespoons salt-cured capers, rinsed

1 cup (100 g) green olives, pitted and coarsely chopped

1 small bunch fresh basil, torn

2 tablespoons finely chopped fresh parsley

1 tablespoon finely chopped fresh oregano

Serves 4-6 • Preparation 30 minutes + 1 hour to drain • Cooking 20-30 minutes • Difficulty 2

1. Put the eggplant slices in a colander and sprinkle with the coarse sea salt. Let drain for 1 hour. Chop into cubes. Heat the frying oil in a large frying pan. Fry the eggplant until golden brown, about 5 minutes. Drain on paper towels.

2. Broil (grill) the bell peppers under an overhead broiler until the skins are blackened. Place in a plastic bag, shut tight, and let rest for 10 minutes. Peel and cut into small squares.

3. Heat 2 tablespoons of extra-virgin olive oil in a small pan over low heat. Add the onion, garlic, and a pinch of salt and simmer until golden, about 15 minutes.

4. Cook the pasta in a large pot of salted boiling water until al dente. Drain well and let cool under cold running water. Drain again and dry on a clean kitchen towel.

5. Put the pasta in a large serving bowl with the eggplant, capers, bell peppers, onions, pine nuts, olives, basil, parsley, and oregano. Toss gently and serve.

Replace the brown rice in this recipe with the same weight of whole-wheat (wholemeal) pasta, pearl barley, farro, or quinoa for an equally delicious salad. Add a touch of sweetness with 2-3 tablespoons raisins or candied (glacé) ginger, mango, or pineapple.

# BROWN RICE SALAD with apples & walnuts

1½  cups (350 g) brown rice
6  tablespoons (90 ml) extra-virgin olive oil
2  tart green organic apples, such as Granny Smiths, unpeeled and coarsely chopped
24  walnuts, coarsely chopped
5  ounces (150 g) g Gruyère or Swiss cheese, cut into small cubes
   Freshly squeezed juice of 1 lemon
1  tablespoon honey, heated
2  cloves garlic, finely chopped
   Salt and freshly ground black pepper
3  tablespoons finely chopped fresh parsley

Serves 4 • Preparation 15 minutes + 30 minutes to cool • Cooking 35-40 minutes • Difficulty 1

1. Cook the rice in 2 quarts (2 liters) of salted boiling water until tender, 35-40 minutes. Drain thoroughly and transfer to a large bowl. Toss with 1 tablespoon of oil and let cool completely, about 30 minutes.

2. Mix the rice with the apples, walnuts, and cheese.

3. Whisk the remaining 5 tablespoons of oil, lemon juice, honey, garlic, and salt and pepper and drizzle over the rice mixture. Sprinkle with the parsley and serve.

If you liked this recipe, you will love these as well.

**APPLE SALAD** with yogurt

**ARUGULA** with red apple, walnuts & parmesan

**FARRO SALAD** with apples, gorgonzola & honey

# BROWN RICE SALAD with veggies & cheese

1½ cups (300 g) brown rice

4 tablespoons (60 ml) extra-virgin olive oil

14 ounces (400 g) green beans, trimmed

1 cucumber, peeled and thinly sliced

20 cherry tomatoes, halved

5 ounces (150 g) Fontina cheese, cut into small cubes

1 bunch fresh parsley, finely chopped

2 tablespoons finely chopped fresh cilantro (coriander)

2 tablespoons freshly squeezed lemon juice

Salt and freshly ground black pepper

Serves 4 • Preparation 20 minutes + 30 minutes to cool • Cooking 35–40 minutes • Difficulty 1

1. Cook the rice in 2 quarts (2 liters) of salted boiling water until tender, 35–40 minutes. Drain thoroughly and transfer to a large bowl. Toss with 1 tablespoon of oil and let cool completely, about 30 minutes.

2. Cook the green beans in salted boiling water until just tender, about 5 minutes. Drain and set aside to cool.

3. Put the cucumber in a colander. Sprinkle with salt and let drain for 15 minutes.

4. Mix the rice, beans, tomatoes, cucumber, cheese, parsley, and cilantro in a bowl. Drizzle with the remaining oil and lemon juice. Season with salt and pepper. Toss gently and serve.

# RICE SALAD with tuna & avocado

2 cups (400 g) short-grain rice
4 tablespoons (60 ml) extra-virgin olive oil
1 small bunch of arugula (rocket), shredded
12 ounces (350 g) canned tuna, drained and crumbled
1 avocado, peeled, pitted, and thinly sliced
8 ounces (250 g) bocconcini (mozzarella balls)
2 tablespoons finely chopped fresh parsley
  Freshly squeezed juice of 1 lemon
  Salt

1. Cook the rice in 2 quarts (2 liters) of salted boiling water until tender, about 15 minutes. Drain and cool under cold running water. Drain well and dry in a clean towel.

2. Transfer to a salad dish and drizzle with 1 tablespoon of oil. Top with the arugula, tuna, avocado, mozzarella, and parsley.

3. Whisk the lemon juice, remaining oil, and salt in a small bowl. Pour over the salad, toss gently, and serve.

Low in saturated fat and calories, shrimp are a good source of protein, vitamin B12, niacin, selenium, iron, phosphorus, and zinc. This salad can also be made with brown rice.

# RICE SALAD with shrimp & arugula

| | |
|---|---|
| 2 | cups (400 g) short-grain rice |
| 1<sup>1</sup>/<sub>2</sub> | pounds (750 g) shrimp (prawns), in shell |
| | Freshly squeezed juice of 1<sup>1</sup>/<sub>2</sub> lemons |
| 6 | tablespoons (90 ml) extra-virgin olive oil |
| | Salt and freshly ground white pepper |
| 4 | tablespoons coarsely chopped arugula (rocket) |

Serves 4-6 • Preparation 15 minutes + 15 minutes to cool • Cooking 15 minutes • Difficulty 1

1. Cook the rice in 2 quarts (2 liters) of salted boiling water until tender, about 15 minutes. Drain and pass under cold running water. Drain again and dry in a clean kitchen towel.

2. Cook the shrimp in 6 cups (1.5 liters) of salted boiling water and the juice of 1 lemon until pink, 3-4 minutes. Drain and let cool.

3. Shell the shrimp. Chop off the heads and rinse thoroughly in cold running water. Transfer to a salad bowl with 4 tablespoons (60 ml) of oil.

4. Add the rice to the bowl with the shrimp. Season with salt and pepper. Add the remaining lemon juice and 2 tablespoons of oil and toss gently. Add the arugula and toss again just before serving.

If you liked this recipe, you will love these as well.

**SHRIMP SALAD**
with back rice

**SHRIMP SALAD**
with lime & lemongrass

**SHRIMP & AVOCADO**
salad

# MIXED RICE SALAD with dried apricots

### Salad

| | |
|---|---|
| 1/2 | cup (100 g) wild rice |
| 1/2 | cup (100 g) brown rice |
| 1/2 | cup (100 g) basmati rice |
| 4 | tablespoons snipped fresh chives |
| 2 | tablespoons finely chopped fresh parsley |
| 8–12 | dried apricots, coarsely chopped |
| 1 | cup (120 g) walnuts, coarsely chopped |

### Dressing

| | |
|---|---|
| 3 | tablespoons walnut oil |
| 3 | tablespoons extra-virgin olive oil |
| 2 | tablespoons white wine vinegar |
| 1 | tablespoon freshly squeezed lemon juice |
| 1/2 | teaspoon light brown sugar |
| 1 | teaspoon Dijon mustard |
| | Salt and freshly ground black pepper |

Serves 4 • Preparation 20 minutes + 30 minutes to cool • Cooking 35–40 minutes • Difficulty 1

## Salad

1. Cook the three types of rice in separate pans of salted boiling water until just tender. Follow the cooking times suggested on each package.

2. Drain each type of rice and let cool, about 30 minutes.

3. Combine the three types of rice in a salad bowl. Add the chives, parsley, apricots, and walnuts and mix well.

## Dressing

1. Whisk both types of oil, the vinegar, lemon juice, sugar, and mustard in a small bowl. Season with salt and pepper.

2. Drizzle the dressing over the salad. Toss gently and serve.

# WILD RICE SALAD with dried fruit

**Salad**

| | |
|---|---|
| 2 | cups (400 g) wild rice |
| 2 | organic oranges |
| 8-12 | dried apricots, coarsely chopped |
| 1/2 | cup (80 g) salted pistachio nuts, toasted |
| 3 | tablespoons finely chopped fresh cilantro (coriander) |

**Dressing**

| | |
|---|---|
| 6 | tablespoons (90 ml) extra-virgin olive oil |
| 2 | tablespoons freshly squeezed lemon or lime juice |
| 1/2 | teaspoon light brown sugar |
| 1 | teaspoon Dijon mustard |
| | Salt and freshly ground black pepper |

Serves 4–6 • Preparation 20 minutes + 30 minutes to cool • Cooking 40 minutes • Difficulty 1

## Salad

1. Cook the wild rice in a large pan of salted boiling water until just tender, about 40 minutes (or the time indicated on the package). Drain well and let cool, about 30 minutes

2. Finely grate the zest from the oranges into a large bowl. Peel and segment the oranges, catching any drips. Place the segments and juice in the bowl with the zest. Mix in the rice, apricots, pistachios, and cilantro.

## Dressing

1. Whisk the oil, lemon juice, sugar, and mustard in a small bowl. Season with salt and pepper.

2. Drizzle the dressing over the salad. Toss gently and serve.

Polished, or pearl barley, as it is usually known, has a pleasant chewy texture and a lovely nutty flavor. It is a good source of iron and dietary fiber. Often used in soups, it works very well in salads too.

# BARLEY SALAD with tuna & mozzarella

12  ounces (350 g) pearl barley
24  cherry tomatoes, halved
1   sweet red onion, finely chopped
8   ounces (250 g) canned tuna, drained
5   ounces (150 g) mozzarella balls
    Salt and freshly ground black pepper
1/4 cup (60 ml) extra-virgin olive oil
    Handful of fresh basil leaves, to garnish

Serves 6–8 • Preparation 20 minutes + 1 hour to chill • Difficulty 1

1. Cook the barley in a large pot of salted boiling water until tender, 35–40 minutes. Drain well and cool under cold running water. Drain again and transfer to a clean kitchen cloth. Dry well and place in a large salad bowl.

2. Add the tomatoes, onion, tuna, and mozzarella. Season with salt and pepper and toss well. Drizzle with the oil, toss again, and serve garnished with the basil.

If you liked this recipe, you will love these as well.

**PASTA SALAD** with tuna, cherry tomatoes & olives

**RICE SALAD** with tuna & avocado

**TUNA & KIDNEY BEAN** salad

# BULGUR SALAD with tomatoes, walnuts & feta

2    cups (300 g) bulgur

4    ounces (120 g) shelled walnuts

1    teaspoon salt

1    sweet red onion, finely chopped

24    cherry tomatoes, halved

4    ounces (120 g) feta cheese, cubed

2    tablespoons finely chopped fresh mint + extra to garnish

1/3    cup (90 ml) extra-virgin olive oil

2    tablespoons freshly squeezed lime juice

Serves 4–6 • Preparation 20 minutes + 30 minutes to rest & chill
Difficulty 1

1. Soak the bulgur in warm water for 15 minutes. Drain, squeezing out the excess water.

2. Chop the walnuts and salt coarsely on a chopping board.

3. Mix the bulgur, walnuts, onion, tomatoes, cheese, and mint in a large bowl. Drizzle with the oil and lime juice. Refrigerate for 15 minutes. Garnish with the mint and serve.

# FARRO SALAD with apples, gorgonzola & honey

2 cups (400 g) farro (or pearl barely)

¹/₂ cup (125 ml) extra-virgin olive oil

3 tablespoons honey

2 tablespoons white wine vinegar

Salt and freshly ground black pepper

2 cups (100 g) baby arugula (rocket) leaves

2 Granny Smith apples, with peel, cored and diced

5 ounces (150 g) spicy Gorgonzola cheese, cubed

Serves 8 • Preparation 20 minutes + 30 minutes to cool • Cooking 40 minutes • Difficulty 1

1. Boil the farro in plenty of salted water until tender, about 45 minutes (or the time indicated on the package). Drain and transfer to a large serving bowl. Let cool, about 30 minutes.

2. Whisk the oil in a small bowl with the vinegar, honey, a pinch of salt, and a generous grinding of black pepper.

3. Add the arugula, apples, and cheese to the bowl with the farro. Drizzle with the honey dressing, toss gently, and serve.

This is an old peasant recipe from Tuscany, in central Italy. It dates back to times when bread was precious and never a crumb was wasted. Serve by itself as a light lunch or supper dish, or as a starter before a traditional meal of roast meat and vegetables. It goes beautifully with a glass of red wine.

# PANZANELLA
## (Tuscan bread salad)

| | |
|---|---|
| 1 | pound (500 g) day-old, firm-textured bread, preferably unsalted |
| 4 | ripe tomatoes, cut into small wedges |
| 1 | large cucumber, peeled and thinly sliced |
| 1 | medium red onion, thinly sliced |
| 2 | tablespoons coarsely chopped fresh basil + extra, to garnish |
| 6 | tablespoons (90 ml) extra-virgin olive oil |
| 2 | tablespoons red wine vinegar |
| | Salt and freshly ground black pepper |

Serves 4-6 • Preparation 20 minutes + 2 hours to rest • Difficulty 1

1. Slice the bread fairly thickly or break it into small chunks. Soak in a bowl of cold water for 5 minutes. Drain the bread in a colander and gently squeeze out all the excess moisture. It should be damp (but not mushy) and crumbly.

2. Transfer the bread to a salad bowl. Add the tomatoes, cucumber, onion, basil, oil, vinegar, salt, and pepper. Toss gently. Let rest at cool room temperature for 2 hours before serving.

3. Garnish with the extra basil and serve.

If you liked this recipe, you will love these as well.

**PASTA SALAD** with tomatoes, feta & olives

**PASTA SALAD** with cheese

**FATTOUSH** (Levantine bread salad)

# COUSCOUS SALAD with eggplant

8 tablespoons (125 ml) extra-virgin olive oil

2 medium eggplants (aubergines), cut into cubes

Salt and freshly ground black pepper

2 cups (300 g) couscous

3 cups (750 ml) boiling water

2 scallions (spring onions), thinly sliced

2 tablespoons fresh basil + extra, to garnish

4 ripe tomatoes, finely chopped

2 tablespoons finely chopped fresh cilantro (coriander)

1 cup (125 g) freshly grated Ricotta salata or Parmesan cheese

Serves 4–6 • Preparation 15 minutes + 10 minutes to stand • Cooking 5–10 minutes • Difficulty 1

1. Heat 4 tablespoons (60 ml) of oil in a large frying pan over medium heat. Add the eggplants and sauté until tender, 5–10 minutes. Remove from the heat, season with salt and pepper, and let cool slightly.

2. Put the couscous in a large bowl. Pour in the water and 1 tablespoon of oil. Season with salt. Mix well and let rest for 10 minutes. Fluff with a fork to separate the grains. Add the scallions and basil.

3. Transfer the couscous to a salad bowl. Add the eggplant, tomatoes, cilantro, and cheese. Drizzle with the remaining 3 tablespoons of oil, garnish with the basil, and serve.

# COUSCOUS SALAD with apple

2 cups (300 g) couscous

3 cups (750 ml) boiling water

4 tablespoons (60 ml) extra-virgin olive oil

Salt

2 organic green apples, cored, and cut into cubes

8 ounces (250 g) Asiago, Cheddar, or Swiss cheese, cut into cubes

Freshly squeezed juice of $^1/_2$ lemon

1-2 teaspoons finely grated ginger

1 fresh red chile, seeded and finely chopped

2-3 tablespoons finely chopped fresh parsley

Serves 4-6 • Preparation 15 minutes + 10 minutes to stand • Difficulty 1

1. Put the couscous in a large bowl. Pour in the water and 1 tablespoon of oil. Season with salt. Mix well and let rest for 10 minutes. Fluff with a fork to separate the grains.

2. Transfer the couscous to a salad bowl. Add the apples, cheese, remaining 3 tablespoons of oil and lemon juice. Season with salt and mix well. Sprinkle with the ginger, chile, and parsley, toss gently and serve.

# POTATO SALAD with eggs

Serves 4–6 • Preparation 15 minutes + 15 minutes to cool
Cooking 15–20 minutes • Difficulty 1

Salad
| | | | |
|---|---|---|---|
| 1½ | pounds (750 g) new potatoes, sliced | 2 | tablespoons finely chopped fresh parsley |
| 4–6 | hard-boiled eggs | | **Dressing** |
| 8 | slices prosciutto | ½ | cup (125 g) mayonnaise |
| 2 | tablespoons extra-virgin olive oil | 2 | tablespoons freshly squeezed lemon juice |
| 3 | scallions (spring onions), thinly sliced | 2 | teaspoons mustard |
| | | | Salt and freshly ground black pepper |

Salad

1. Boil the potatoes in a large pot of salted water until tender, 10–15 minutes. Drain and let cool, 15 minutes.

2. Sauté the prosciutto in the oil until crisp, about 5 minutes. Break each slice into 2–3 pieces.

3. Toss the potatoes, eggs, prosciutto, scallions, and parsley carefully in a large salad bowl.

Dressing

1. Whisk the mayonnaise, lemon juice, and mustard in a small bowl. Season with salt and pepper. Drizzle over the salad and serve.

# POTATO SALAD with chorizo

Serves 4 • Preparation 15 minutes + 15 minutes to cool
Cooking 10–15 minutes • Difficulty 1

| | | | |
|---|---|---|---|
| 1 | pound (500 g) waxy potatoes, thickly sliced | | leaves separated |
| 8 | ounces (250 g) Spanish chorizo sausage, thinly sliced lengthwise | 4 | hard-boiled eggs, halved |
| 1 | head red radicchio, | ¾ | cup (180 ml) light mayonnaise |

1. Boil the potatoes in a large pot of salted water until tender, 10–15 minutes. Drain and let cool, about 15 minutes.

2. Dry-fry the sausage in a large frying pan over high heat until crisp, 4–5 minutes.

3. Combine the potatoes, sausage, and radicchio in a large salad bowl. Top with the eggs.

4. Add the mayonnaise and stir carefully. Serve at once.

# NEW POTATO salad

Serves 4–6 • Preparation 15 minutes + 15 minutes to cool
Cooking 15–20 minutes • Difficulty 1

| | | | |
|---|---|---|---|
| 2 | pounds (1 kg) small new potatoes | 1 | tablespoon horseradish cream |
| ½ | cup (125 g) plain yogurt | 1 | bunch fresh chives, snipped |
| ¼ | cup (60 ml) extra-virgin olive oil | | |

1. Boil the potatoes in a large pot of salted water until tender, 10–15 minutes. Drain and let cool, about 15 minutes.

2. Whisk the yogurt, horseradish cream, and oil in a large bowl.

3. Add the potatoes to the bowl with the yogurt dressing, mixing well. Add the chives . Toss gently and serve.

# LEMON POTATO salad

Serves 4–6 • Preparation 15 minutes + 1 hour 30 minutes to cool & chill • Cooking 20–25 minutes • Difficulty 1

| | | | |
|---|---|---|---|
| 6 | medium potatoes | | chopped |
| 2 | tablespoons finely chopped fresh parsley | | Freshly squeezed juice of 1 lemon |
| 2 | scallions (spring onions), finely chopped | ½ | cup (125 ml) extra-virgin olive oil |
| 1 | clove garlic, finely | | |

1. Boil the potatoes in their skins in a large pot of salted water until tender, 20–25 minutes. Drain and let cool, about 30 minutes. Slip off the skins and cut into small cubes.

2. Mix the potatoes, parsley, and scallions in a large salad bowl.

3. Whisk the garlic, lemon juice, and oil in a small bowl.

4. Pour over the potatoes and toss well. Refrigerate for at least 1 hour before serving.

Fattoush is a bread salad from the Levant, made by tearing yesterday's pita breads into bite-size pieces and garnishing with a mixture seasonal salad vegetables and herbs. Vary the ingredients according to what you have on hand. Lemon-flavored sumac is a traditional ingredient. It is available in Middle Eastern food stores.

# FATTOUSH
## (Levantine bread salad)

| | |
|---|---|
| 4–6 | day-old pita breads |
| 1 | cucumber, cut in small cubes |
| 3 | firm-ripe tomatoes, cut in small cubes |
| 1 | onion, finely chopped |
| 1 | small bunch fresh parsley, finely chopped |
| 1 | small bunch fresh mint, finely chopped |
| 1 | small bunch fresh cilantro (coriander) finely chopped |
| 2 | cloves garlic, finely chopped |
| | Freshly squeezed juice of 2 lemons |
| $^1/_2$ | cup (125 ml) extra-virgin olive oil |
| | Salt and freshly ground white pepper |
| 1 | teaspoon sumac |
| | Seeds from 1 pomegranate |

Serves 4–6 • Preparation 25 minutes • Cooking 5–10 minutes Difficulty: 1

1. Preheat the oven to 350°F (180°C/gas 4). Tear the pita bread into bite-size pieces. Toast in the oven for 5–10 minutes, until golden brown and crisp.

2. Transfer to a large bowl and mix in the cucumber, tomatoes, onion, parsley, mint, cilantro, and garlic. Drizzle with the lemon juice and oil and toss well. Season with salt, pepper, and sumac.

3. Sprinkle with the pomegranate seeds and serve.

If you liked this recipe, you will love these as well.

**ORANGE & WATERCRESS** salad

**BULGUR SALAD** with tomatoes, walnuts & feta

**PANZANELLA** (Tuscan bread salad)

# seafood salads

## SHRIMP SALAD with black rice

| | |
|---|---|
| ¹/₂ | organic lemon |
| 12 | ounces (350 g) shelled shrimp (prawns), heads removed |
| 1 | scallion (spring onion), thinly sliced |
| 2 | cloves garlic, finely chopped |
| 4 | tablespoons (60 ml) extra-virgin olive oil |
| | Salt and freshly ground black pepper |
| 2 | cups (400 g) black rice |
| 20 | cherry tomatoes, halved |
| 1 | small bunch fresh parsley, finely chopped |

Serves 6 • Preparation 30 minutes + 15 minutes to marinate • Cooking 20 minutes • Difficulty 2

1. Squeeze the juice from the lemon and set aside. Use a sharp knife to remove the yellow zest and slice thinly.

2. Combine the shrimp in a large bowl with the scallion, garlic, lemon zest and juice, 2 tablespoons of oil, and a grinding of pepper. Mix well and let marinate for 15 minutes.

3. Cook the rice in 2 quarts (2 liters) of salted boiling water for the time indicated on the package. Put under cold running water, drain well, and dry on a clean cloth.

4. Heat the remaining 2 tablespoons of oil in a large frying pan over high heat and sauté the cherry tomatoes for 1–2 minutes. Season with salt and pepper, add the shrimp and marinade, and cook until tender, 2–3 minutes.

5. Transfer the rice to a large bowl and top with the shrimp mixture. Sprinkle with the parsley and serve.

If you liked this recipe, you will love these as well.

**RICE SALAD**
with tuna & avocado

**RICE SALAD**
with shrimp & arugula

**BARLEY SALAD**
with tuna & mozzarella

# SALMON & GARBANZO BEAN salad

| | |
|---|---|
| 1 | (8-ounce/250-g) can pink salmon, drained and flaked |
| 1 | (14-ounce/400-g) can garbanzo beans (chickpeas), drained and rinsed |
| 2 | cucumbers, halved and sliced |
| 1 | red onion, thinly sliced |
| 3 | cups (150 g) baby spinach leaves |
| | Salt and freshly ground black pepper |
| ½ | cup (125 ml) plain yogurt |
| 2 | tablespoons freshly squeezed lemon juice |
| 1 | tablespoon tahini (sesame paste) |
| 1 | tablespoon finely chopped fresh chives |

Serves 2-4 • Preparation 10 minutes • Difficulty 1

1.  Mix the salmon, garbanzo beans, cucumbers, red onion, and spinach in a large bowl. Toss well. Season with salt and pepper.

2.  Whisk the yogurt, lemon juice, tahini, and chives in a small bowl.

3.  Spoon the salad onto serving plates, drizzle with the dressing, and serve.

# TUNA & KIDNEY BEAN salad

1 (8-ounce/250-g) can tuna, drained
1 (14-ounce/400-g) can red kidney beans, drained
1 sweet red onion, sliced
2 tablespoons finely chopped fresh parsley
1 tablespoon finely chopped fresh cilantro (coriander)
1 small lettuce
1/4 cup (60 ml) extra-virgin olive oil
2 teaspoon Dijon mustard
  Freshly squeezed juice of 1 lemon
  Salt and freshly ground black pepper

1. Put the tuna in a medium bowl and break it up with a fork. Add the beans, onion, parsley, and cilantro and toss well.

2. Arrange the lettuce leaves so that they line the base and sides of a medium salad bowl. Spoon the bean and tuna mixture into the lettuce leaves.

3. Whisk the oil, mustard, lemon juice, salt, and pepper in a small bowl. Drizzle over the salad and serve.

A fresh seafood salad is one of the healthiest meals you can prepare. Depending on which ingredients you chose, it will be low in calories but rich in lean protein, omega-3 oils, vitamin B12, and zinc.

**78**

# SEAFOOD salad

| | |
|---|---|
| 1 | pound (500 g) mussels, in shell |
| 14 | ounces (400 g) shrimp (prawns) |
| 2 | cloves garlic, finely chopped |
| 4 | tablespoons (60 ml) extra-virgin olive oil |
| 14 | ounces (400 g) firm white fish fillets, such as cod or sea bass |
| 14 | ounces (400 g) baby octopus, cleaned |
| 1 | tablespoon white wine vinegar |
| 1 | tablespoon freshly squeezed lemon juice |
| | Salt |
| 1 | large onion, finely sliced, soaked in cold water for 10 minutes, drained |
| 1 | head celery, finely chopped |
| 1 | (14-ounce/400-g) can cannellini beans, drained |

Serves 4-6 • Preparation 30 minutes + 1 hour to soak • Cooking 40-50 minutes • Difficulty 2

1. Soak the mussels in cold water for 1 hour. Scrub well, pulling off any beards. Cook in a large pot over medium heat until they open, 5–10 minutes. Discard any that do not open. Shell and set aside.

2. Cook the shrimp with the garlic and 1 tablespoon of oil in a large saucepan over medium heat for 2 minutes. Shell and let cool.

3. Steam the fish fillets until tender, 3–5 minutes Let cool.

4. Cook the octopus in 2 cups (500 ml) of salted boiling water, 1 tablespoon of oil, and the vinegar over medium heat until tender, about 30 minutes. Drain and chop coarsely.

5. Whisk the lemon juice, remaining 2 tablespoons of oil, and salt in a small bowl. Put the mussels, shrimp, fish fillets, octopus, onion, celery, and beans on a large salad platter or in individual salad bowls. Drizzle with the oil mixture. Refrigerate until ready to serve.

If you liked this recipe, you will love these as well.

**84**

SHRIMP, SCALLOP
& ARUGULA salad

**88**

SEAFOOD SALAD
with grapefruit

**92**

SEAFOOD & POTATO
salad

# SALMON & AVOCADO salad

Serves 4 • Preparation 10–15 minutes • Cooking 5 minutes
Difficulty 1

| | | | |
|---|---|---|---|
| 2 | tablespoons sesame seeds | 2 | medium ripe avocados, peeled, pitted, and sliced |
| 1/4 | cup (60 ml) mirin | 5 | cups (250 g) baby spinach leaves |
| 1/4 | cup (60 ml) soy sauce | 12 | ounces (350 g) smoked salmon, thinly sliced |
| 2 | tablespoons vegetable oil | | |
| 1 | tablespoon sugar | | |

1. Dry-fry the sesame seeds in a small frying pan over medium heat until browned, about 2 minutes. Remove from the heat and set aside.

2. Mix the mirin, soy sauce, oil, and sugar in a small saucepan. Bring to a boil over medium-high heat, stirring until the sugar has dissolved. Boil for 1 minute. Let cool slightly.

3. Arrange the spinach and avocado on individual serving plates. Top with the smoked salmon. Drizzle with the warm soy dressing. Sprinkle with the sesame seeds and serve.

# TUNA & ROAST VEGGIE salad

Serves 4 • Preparation 10 minutes • Cooking 20 minutes
Difficulty 1

| | | | |
|---|---|---|---|
| 2 | red onions, cut into thick wedges | 2 | tablespoons extra-virgin olive oil |
| 1 | yellow bell pepper (capsicum), seeded, and cut into strips | 1 | tablespoon balsamic vinegar |
| 1 | red bell pepper (capsicum), seeded, and cut into strips | | Salt and freshly ground black pepper |
| 1 | pound (500 g) cherry tomatoes | 1 | cup (100 g) black olives |
| | | 1 | (14-ounce/400-g) can tuna, drained |

1. Preheat the oven to 450°F (230°C/gas 8). Put the onions, bell peppers, and tomatoes in a large roasting pan. Drizzle with 1 tablespoon of oil and the balsamic vinegar. Season with salt and pepper. Roast for about 20 minutes, until tender.

2. Arrange the vegetables and olives on a serving plate. Top with the tuna and drizzle with the remaining 1 tablespoon of oil. Serve warm.

# TUNA tartare

Serves 6 • Preparation 10–15 minutes • Difficulty 1

| | | | |
|---|---|---|---|
| 1 1/2 | pounds (750 g) yellowfin tuna | 2 | tablespoons salt-cured capers, rinsed |
| 2 | avocados, peeled, halved, and seeded | 1/4 | cup (60 ml) freshly squeezed lemon juice |
| 3 | cups (150 g) watercress | | |

1. Remove the blood line and any bones from the tuna. Dice into 3/4-inch (2-cm) cubes and place in a large salad bowl.

2. Dice the avocados to about the same size and add to the tuna. Add the capers and lemon juice and stir gently to combine.

3. Divide the tuna and watercress evenly among six serving plates and serve.

# CEVICHE with mango

Serves 4 • Preparation 15 minutes + 1 hour to chill
Difficulty 1

| | | | |
|---|---|---|---|
| 2 | pounds (1 kg) skinless firm white fish fillets, such as flounder, snapper, grouper, cod, or trevalla | 3 | small red chiles, seeded and finely chopped |
| 1 | large mango, peeled and diced | 8 | limes, juiced + 1 tablespoon finely chopped lime zest |
| | | | Salt |

1. Cut the fish into 3/4-inch (2-cm) cubes and put into a medium bowl. Add the mango, chiles, lime juice, and zest and stir to combine.

2. Cover the bowl and refrigerate for 1 hour, or until fish turns from opaque to white.

3. Season to taste with salt and serve.

# SHRIMP SALAD with lime & lemongrass

2     stalks lemongrass, thinly sliced

1/2    cup (125 ml) freshly squeezed lime juice

3     tablespoons peanut oil

1 1/2   tablespoons brown or palm sugar

2     teaspoons Asian fish sauce

2     small fresh red chiles, thinly sliced

2     pounds (1 kg) large shrimp (king prawns), peeled and deveined

2     cucumbers, thinly sliced lengthwise

2     scallions (spring onions), thinly sliced

1/2    cup (25 g) fresh cilantro (coriander) leaves

1/2    cup (25 g) fresh mint leaves

1/2    cup (60 g) roasted peanuts, chopped

Serves 6 • Preparation 15 minutes + 10 minutes to marinate • Cooking 5–10 minutes • Difficulty 2

1. Whisk the lemongrass, lime juice, oil, sugar, fish sauce, and chiles in a large bowl. Reserve 1/4 cup (60 ml).

2. Add the shrimp to the remaining mixture. Toss well to coat. Set aside to marinate for 10 minutes.

3. Heat a lightly oiled grill or frying pan over high heat. Cook the shrimp in batches, tossing often, until just cooked through, 2–3 minutes. Transfer to a plate. Keep warm.

4. Combine the cucumbers, scallions, cilantro, and mint in a large bowl. Pour in the reserved lemongrass mixture. Toss to combine. Arrange the shrimp and salad on serving plates. Sprinkle with the roasted peanuts and serve.

# SHRIMP & AVOCADO *salad*

## Dill Dressing

| | |
|---|---|
| 1 | large egg yolk |
| 1 | teaspoon Dijon mustard |
| 1/2 | cup (125 ml) extra-virgin olive oil |
| 2 | teaspoons freshly squeezed lemon juice |
| 2 | tablespoons finely chopped fresh dill |
| 1/4 | cup (60 ml) sour cream |
| | Salt and freshly ground black pepper |

## Salad

| | |
|---|---|
| 1 | head baby romaine (cos) lettuce |
| 24 | cooked large shrimp (prawns), peeled and deveined |
| 2 | avocados, peeled and sliced lengthwise |

Serves 4 • Preparation 10 minutes • Difficulty 2

## Dill Dressing

1. Beat the egg yolk and mustard in a double boiler over barely simmering water with an electric mixer at high speed until pale. Gradually beat in the oil in a thin steady trickle until thick. Add the lemon juice and dill. Stir in the sour cream and season with salt and pepper.

## Salad

1. Arrange the lettuce, shrimp, and avocados on individual serving plates. Drizzle with the dill dressing and serve.

If liked, drizzle this salad with 2 tablespoons of freshly squeezed lime juice along with the final drizzling of oil. These quantities will make a light lunch for two or a starter for four.

# SHRIMP, SCALLOP & ARUGULA salad

| | |
|---|---|
| 12 | large shrimp (prawns), heads removed |
| 4 | tablespoons (60 ml) extra-virgin olive oil |
| 6 | scallops, shucked |
| 1 | clove garlic, peeled and lightly crushed |
| 3 | cups (150 g) arugula (rocket) leaves |
| 12 | cherry tomatoes, quartered |
| | Salt and freshly ground black pepper |

Serves 2–4 • Preparation 15 minutes • Cooking 4–6 minutes • Difficulty 1

1. Cook the shrimp in a large pot of salted boiling water until pink, 2–3 minutes. Drain and let cool. Remove the shells and devein.

2. Heat 2 tablespoons of oil in a medium saucepan over medium heat. Add the scallops and garlic and cook until the scallops turn opaque, 2–3 minutes.

3. Divide the arugula between among two to four serving dishes and top with the shrimp, scallops, and tomatoes. Season with salt and pepper and drizzle with the remaining 2 tablespoons of oil. Serve warm.

If you liked this recipe, you will love these as well.

**SHRIMP SALAD**
with lime & lemongrass

**SHRIMP & AVOCADO**
salad

**SHRIMP COCKTAIL**
with mango

# SHRIMP COCKTAIL with mango

¾ cup (180 ml) mayonnaise

¼ cup (60 ml) freshly squeezed lime juice

1½ pounds (750 g) cooked shrimp (prawn), peeled and deveined

2 mangos, peeled and diced

1 small head romaine (cos) lettuce

Serves 4 • Preparation 15 minutes • Difficulty 1

1. Combine the mayonnaise and lime juice in a large bowl. Add the shrimp and mangos and stir well to combine.

2. Coarsely shred the lettuce and divide among four serving bowls. If preferred, use whole leaves.

3. Top with the shrimp mixture and serve.

# NIÇOISE salad

## Salad

6   medium firm-ripe tomatoes, cut into eight wedges

Coarse sea salt

2   cups (100 g) mixed salad greens

1   red bell pepper (capsicum), seeded, cored, and cut into thin strips

1³/₄ cups (200 g) canned tuna in oil, drained

3   stalks celery, finely chopped

3   shallots, finely chopped

8   black olives

8   anchovy fillets in oil

2   hard-boiled eggs, quartered

## Dressing

¹/₂  cup (120 ml) extra-virgin olive oil

2   tablespoons white wine vinegar

Salt and freshly ground black pepper

Serves 4 • Preparation 15 minutes + 1 hour to drain • Difficulty 1

## Salad

1. Put the tomatoes in a colander and sprinkle with salt. Let drain for 1 hour.

2. Arrange the salad greens in four individual serving dishes. Top with the tomatoes, bell pepper, tuna, celery, and shallots in the center.

3. Wrap the olives up in the anchovy fillets and arrange on top. Top with the wedges of egg.

## Dressing

1. Whisk the oil and vinegar in a small bowl. Season with salt and pepper. Drizzle over the salads and serve.

Low in calories and high in nutritional value, this salad makes a wonderful light lunch.

**88**

# SEAFOOD SALAD with grapefruit

| | |
|---|---|
| 12 | large shrimp (prawns), shelled |
| 20 | large clams, in shell |
| 1 | large grapefruit |
| 2 | cups (100 g) arugula (rocket) |
| 6 | button mushrooms, thinly sliced |
| $1/3$ | cup (90 ml) extra-virgin olive oil |
| | Salt and freshly ground black pepper |

Serves 2 • Preparation 15 minutes • Cooking 12-15 minutes • Difficulty 2

1. Cook the shrimp in a large pot of salted, boiling water for 2-3 minutes. Drain and let cool.

2. Cook the clams in a medium saucepan over high heat until they open, 5-10 minutes. Discard any that do not open. Remove the clams from the shells.

3. Use a sharp knife to peel the grapefruit. Cut it into segments, collecting the juice in a small bowl.

4. Divide the arugula between two serving bowls. Top with the mushrooms, grapefruit, shrimp, and clams.

5. Add the oil to the bowl with the grapefruit juice. Season with salt and pepper and whisk to combine.

6. Drizzle over the salads and serve.

If you liked this recipe, you will love these as well.

**BABY SPINACH** with grapefruit & parmesan

**SEAFOOD** salad

**SHRIMP COCKTAIL** with mango

# CRAB SALAD with fennel

### Dressing

| | |
|---|---|
| 2 | large tomatoes |
| 5 | tablespoons (75 ml) extra-virgin olive oil |
| ¼ | cup (60 ml) light (single) cream |
| 1 | tablespoon white wine vinegar |
| 1 | teaspoon finely chopped fresh tarragon |
| | Dash of Worcestershire sauce |
| | Pinch of sugar |
| | Salt and freshly ground black pepper |
| 1 | (2-inch/5-cm) piece cucumber, peeled and diced |

### Salad

| | |
|---|---|
| 8 | ounces (250 g) crabmeat |
| 1 | large bulb fennel, thinly sliced |
| 2 | cups (100 g) mixed salad greens |
| 1 | tablespoon snipped fresh chives |
| | Sweet paprika, to dust |

Serves 2 • Preparation 15 minutes • Difficulty 1

## Dressing

1. Put the tomatoes in a bowl and cover with boiling water. Leave for 30 seconds then remove the skins. Cut in half, squeezing out as many seeds as possible. Cut into small squares.

2. Whisk the oil, cream, vinegar, tarragon, Worcestershire sauce, sugar, salt, and pepper in a small bowl. Stir in the tomatoes and cucumber.

## Salad

1. Mix the crabmeat and fennel in a medium bowl then stir in half the dressing.

2. Arrange the salad greens on four serving plates and top with the crab mixture. Spoon the remaining dressing over the top. Sprinkle with chives, dust with paprika, and serve.

# GRILLED BABY OCTOPUS *salad*

12 ounces (350 g) fresh baby octopus or calamari, cleaned

1/3 cup (90 ml) Thai sweet chili sauce

2 tablespoons freshly squeezed lime juice

1 tablespoon Thai fish sauce

1 tablespoon sesame oil

2 cups (100 g) mixed salad greens

1 cup (50 g) bean sprouts

1 cucumber, with peel, thinly sliced

8 ounces (250 g) cherry tomatoes, halved

1/2 cup (25 g) coarsely chopped fresh cilantro (coriander)

Lime wedges, to serve

Serves 4 • Preparation 15 minutes + 4–12 hours to marinate • Cooking 5–10 minutes • Difficulty 2

1. Put the octopus in a glass or ceramic bowl. Whisk the sweet chili sauce, lime juice, fish sauce, and sesame oil in a small bowl. Pour over the octopus, cover, and marinate for 4 hours or overnight. Drain and reserve the marinade.

2. Divide the salad greens evenly among four serving plates. Top with the bean sprouts, cucumber, and tomatoes.

3. Preheat a barbecue plate or grill pan to very hot. Add the octopus all at once and toss until cooked through, 2–3 minutes. Remove and set aside. Do not overcook.

4. Put the marinade in a small saucepan and bring to a boil.

5. Arrange the octopus on top of the salads. Drizzle with the hot marinade and garnish with the cilantro and lime wedges. Serve at once.

# SEAFOOD & POTATO salad

## Salad

| | |
|---|---|
| 2 | large potatoes, peeled and sliced |
| 12 | ounces (350 g) shrimp (prawns), heads removed and shelled |
| 12 | mussels, shelled |
| 1 | romaine (cos) lettuce, coarsely sliced |
| 1 | stalk celery, sliced |
| 1 | medium-size cooked squid, sliced |
| 6–8 | radishes, sliced |

Salt and freshly ground black pepper

## Dressing

| | |
|---|---|
| $1/2$ | cup (120 ml) light mayonnaise |
| 2 | tablespoons plain yogurt |
| | Freshly squeezed juice of 1 lemon |
| 1 | tablespoon finely chopped fresh parsley |
| 2 | scallions (spring onions), sliced |
| 2 | tablespoons extra-virgin olive oil |

Salt and freshly ground black pepper

Serves 4 • Preparation 20 minutes • Difficulty 1

## Salad

1. Cook the potatoes in salted boiling water until tender, 8–10 minutes. Drain well.

2. Cook the shrimp in salted boiling water until pink, 2–3 minutes. Drain well. Boil the mussels in a small pot of lightly salted water for 2–3 minutes. Drain well.

3. Line the bottom of a salad bowl or serving platter with the potatoes. Cover with the lettuce and celery and top with the shrimp, squid, and mussels. Sprinkle with the radishes. Season lightly with salt and pepper.

## Dressing

1. Whisk the mayonnaise, yogurt, lemon juice, scallions, parsley, oil, salt, and pepper in a small bowl.

2. Drizzle the dressing over the salad and serve.

If you liked this recipe, you will love these as well.

**POTATO SALAD**
with eggs

**SEAFOOD**
salad

**SEAFOOD SALAD**
with grapefruit

# WARM SALAD with monkfish & shrimp

| | |
|---|---|
| 5 | tablespoons (75 ml) extra-virgin olive oil |
| | Salt |
| 1 | tablespoon freshly squeezed lemon juice |
| $^1/_2$ | teaspoon crushed black peppercorns |
| $^1/_2$ | teaspoon crushed fennel seeds |
| $^1/_2$ | teaspoon crushed red pepper flakes |
| 4 | ounces (125 g) thin monkfish fillets, membranes removed |
| 12 | jumbo shrimp (prawns), peeled and deveined |
| 3 | tablespoons sherry vinegar |
| $^1/_2$ | cup (125 g) clarified butter |
| 1 | large tomato, peeled and diced |
| 2 | tablespoons chopped fresh chervil |
| 2 | heads Belgian endive (witlof/chicory) |

Serves 4 • Preparation 30 minutes + 1 hour to marinate • Cooking 10 minutes • Difficulty 2

1. Mix 4 tablespoons (60 ml) of oil, 1 teaspoon salt, lemon juice, peppercorns, fennel seeds, and red pepper in a bowl. Add the monkfish, turning to coat. Let marinate for 1 hour.

2. Heat the remaining 1 tablespoon of oil in a large frying pan over high heat. Take the fish out of the marinade and cook until lightly browned, 2 minutes on each side. Set aside.

3. Add the shrimp to the pan and toss over high heat until cooked through and lightly browned, about 2 minutes. Remove and keep warm.

4. Remove the pan from the heat and add the sherry vinegar and marinade and let it bubble as the heat dissipates. Add the clarified butter, tomato, and chervil.

5. Arrange the endive, fish, and shrimp on four serving plates. Spoon the sherry mixture over the top and serve.

# WARM & SPICY fish salad

## Spice Mix

2   tablespoons sweet paprika
1   teaspoon cayenne pepper
1   teaspoon ground turmeric
1   teaspoon dried oregano
1   teaspoon dried thyme
1/2 teaspoon freshly ground black pepper
1/4 teaspoon ground nutmeg
1   teaspoon sugar
1   teaspoon salt

## Salad

2   cups (100 g) baby spinach
24  cherry tomatoes, halved
1   small red onion, finely sliced
2   tablespoons extra-virgin olive oil
2   tablespoons freshly squeezed lemon juice
1/2 teaspoon Dijon mustard

## Fish

3   tablespoons extra-virgin olive oil
4   (8-ounce/250-g) firm white fish fillets (snapper, cod, halibut, whiting, monkfish)
1   lemon, cut into wedges

Serves 4–6 • Preparation 15 minutes • Cooking 5 minutes • Difficulty 2

## Spice Mix

1.  Mix the paprika, cayenne pepper, turmeric, oregano, thyme, black pepper, nutmeg, sugar, and salt in a small bowl and set aside.

## Salad

1.  Combine the spinach, tomatoes, and onion in a medium bowl and set aside. Whisk the oil, lemon juice, and mustard in a small bowl. Pour the dressing over the salad and toss to combine. Set aside.

## Fish

1.  Preheat a large frying pan over medium-high heat. Brush the fish with oil and coat in the spice mix. Cook until blackened and the flesh flakes easily, 2 minutes each side. Serve hot with the salad and lemon wedges.

# meaty salads

## WARM THAI CHICKEN salad

2    stalks lemongrass, coarsely chopped

4    lime leaves, stalks removed and coarsely chopped

2    red chiles, seeded

3    garlic cloves

1    ($^1\!/_2$-inch/1-cm) piece fresh root ginger

4    skinless boneless chicken breasts

2    tablespoons sesame oil

1    teaspoon chile powder

3    tablespoons Thai fish sauce

1    red onion, chopped

3    tablespoons freshly squeezed lime juice

2    tablespoons coarsely chopped fresh basil

2    tablespoons coarsely chopped fresh mint

2    tablespoons coarsely chopped fresh cilantro (coriander)

2    small romaine (cos) lettuces, leaves separated

1    cucumber, seeds removed and cut into strips lengthways

2    cups (100 g) bean sprouts

     Lime wedges, to serve

Serves 4–6 • Preparation 20 minutes • Cooking 15 minutes • Difficulty 2

1. Combine the lemongrass, lime leaves, chiles, garlic, and ginger in a processor and process until everything is very finely chopped together. Set aside.

2. Put the chicken breasts in the food processor and chop coarsely; leave a little bit of texture in the chicken.

3. Heat a wok over high heat with the sesame oil. Add the lemongrass mixture and stir-fry for 1–2 minutes. Add the chicken and chile powder and stir-fry for 4 minutes.

4. Stir in the fish sauce. Decrease the heat to medium-low and simmer the chicken mixture for 4–5 more minutes, stirring often. Add the onion and cook for 2 minutes.

5. Remove from the heat. Drizzle with the lime juice. Add the basil, mint, cilantro, lettuce, cucumber, and bean sprouts and toss well. Serve warm garnished with the lime wedges.

If you liked this recipe, you will love these as well.

**SPICY TURKEY**
salad

**WARM ORIENTAL CHICKEN** salad

**THAI BEEF**
salad

# WARM CHICKEN salad

3    tablespoons extra-virgin
     olive oil
1    small leek, finely chopped
2    boneless skinless chicken
     breasts, thinly sliced
2    yellow bell peppers
     (capsicums), seeded and
     thinly sliced
1    small carrot, thinly sliced
     Salt
     Finely grated zest of $1/2$ lime
1    tablespoon finely chopped
     fresh cilantro (coriander)
2–3  drops Worcestershire sauce

Serves 4 • Preparation 15 minutes • Cooking 12–15 minutes • Difficulty 1

1.  Heat the oil in a large frying pan over medium heat.
    Add the leek and sauté until softened, 3–4 minutes.

2.  Add the chicken and sauté for 3 minutes. Add the bell
    peppers and carrot. Season with salt. Simmer for 5 minutes,
    stirring often, until the chicken is cooked through.

3.  Stir in the lime zest, cilantro, and Worcestershire sauce.
    Transfer to serving dishes and serve warm.

# CHICKEN & CORN salad

2 boneless skinless chicken breasts, cut in small cubes

¹/₂ cup (75 g) canned or frozen baby corn (sweet corn)

3 tablespoons extra-virgin olive oil

1 tablespoon wholegrain mustard

Salt

3 cups (150 g) mixed salad greens

6 tablespoons chopped walnuts

2 tablespoon finely chopped fresh parsley

Serves 4 • Preparation 10 minutes • Cooking 5–10 minutes • Difficulty 1

1. Steam the chicken until cooked through, 5–10 minutes. Cool under cold running water. Dry well in a clean cloth.

2. Cook the corn in a large pot of salted boiling water until tender, 2–3 minutes. Drain and cool under cold running water. Dry in a clean cloth.

3. Whisk the oil and mustard in a small bowl. Season with salt. Arrange the salad greens in a large bowl. Add the chicken, walnuts, parsley, and corn. Drizzle with the dressing and serve.

This delicious salad makes a very healthy lunch or dinner. You can prepare the chicken and broccoli ahead of time and assemble the salad in minutes.

# CHICKEN SALAD with figs & broccoli

| 3 | tablespoons butter |
| 2 | boneless skinless chicken breasts, thinly sliced |
| 1 | pound (500 g) broccoli, cut into florets |
| | Zest of 1 orange, cut into very thin strips |
| | Zest of 1 lemon, cut into very thin strips |
| | Freshly squeezed juice of $^1/_2$ orange |
| | Salt and freshly ground black pepper |
| $^1/_4$ | cup (60 ml) extra-virgin olive oil |
| 1 | crisp lettuce, washed and finely shredded |
| 6 | figs, cut into segments |

Serves 4 • Preparation 20 minutes + 15 minutes to cool • Cooking 10–15 minutes • Difficulty 1

1. Heat the butter in a large frying pan over medium heat. Add the chicken and sauté until cooked through and lightly browned, 5–10 minutes. Remove from the heat and let cool, about 15 minutes.

2. Cook the broccoli in a large pot of salted boiling water until just tender, about 5 minutes. Drain and rinse under cold running water.

3. Combine the orange and lemon zests in a small bowl. Gently whisk in the orange juice and oil. Season with salt and pepper.

4. Arrange the lettuce on a large serving dish or in four individual salad bowls. Top with the figs, broccoli, and chicken. Drizzle with the orange mixture and serve.

If you liked this recipe, you will love these as well.

**WARM THAI CHICKEN**
salad

**CHICKEN & SUGARSNAP**
salad

**CHICKEN & FRUIT**
salad

# SPICY TURKEY salad

Serves 4 • Preparation 20 minutes + 15 minutes to cool
Cooking 5-10 minutes • Difficulty 1

| | | | |
|---|---|---|---|
| 1/3 | cup (90 ml) chicken stock | 2 | small fresh red chiles, seeded and finely chopped |
| 3 | tablespoons freshly squeezed lime juice | 3 | scallions (spring onions), thinly sliced |
| 1 | stalk lemongrass, trimmed, crushed, and thinly sliced | 1/4 | cup finely chopped fresh cilantro (coriander) |
| 2 | cloves garlic, crushed | 2 | tablespoons finely chopped fresh mint |
| 1 | pound (500 g) ground (minced) turkey | | Crisp lettuce leaves, to serve |
| 1 | tablespoon Asian fish sauce | | |
| 1 | tablespoon sugar | | |

1. Combine the stock, lime juice, lemongrass, and garlic in a frying pan. Bring to a boil over high heat. Add the turkey. Reduce the heat to low and sauté, breaking up the meat with a wooden spoon, until cooked through, about 5 minutes.

2. Stir in the fish sauce and sugar. Set aside to cool for 15 minutes. Stir in the chiles, scallions, cilantro, and mint. Arrange the lettuce leaves in salad bowls. Spoon the turkey mixture over the top and serve.

# SMOKED CHICKEN salad

Serves 4-6 • Preparation 20 minutes • Cooking 5 minutes
Difficulty 1

| | | | |
|---|---|---|---|
| 1 | smoked chicken (about 2 pounds/1 kg) | 3 | tablespoons red wine vinegar |
| 3 | stalks celery, thinly sliced | 1/3 | cup (90 ml) extra-virgin olive or grape seed oil |
| 2 | scallions (green onions), trimmed and thinly sliced | | Salt and freshly ground black pepper |
| 3 | ounces (60 g) snow pea shoots, trimmed | 2 | avocados, peeled, pitted, and sliced |
| 1/3 | cup (90 ml) whole berry cranberry sauce | | |

1. Shred the smoked chicken flesh, discarding the skin and bones. Place in a large bowl. Add the celery, scallions, and snow pea shoots. Toss to combine.

2. Heat the cranberry sauce in a saucepan over medium heat until warm. Pour into a small bowl. Add the vinegar and oil. Season with salt and pepper. Whisk until combined.

3. Arrange the avocados on serving plates. Top with smoked chicken mixture. Drizzle with the cranberry mixture and serve.

# CHICKEN SALAD with yogurt

Serves 4-6 • Preparation 20 minutes + 10 minutes to rest
Cooking 10 minutes • Difficulty 1

| | | | |
|---|---|---|---|
| 4 | boneless, skinless chicken breasts | 1/4 | cup (60 ml) Greek-style yogurt |
| 3 | tablespoons extra-virgin olive oil | 2 | teaspoons honey |
| 1/4 | cup (60 ml) freshly squeezed lime juice | 2 | cucumbers, very thinly sliced lengthwise |
| | Salt and freshly ground black pepper | 1 | small Iceberg lettuce, halved and cut into in thin wedges |
| 1/3 | cup (90 ml) mayonnaise | | |

1. Combine the chicken, oil, 3 tablespoons of lime juice, salt and pepper in a bowl.

2. Heat a grill over medium-high heat. Grill the chicken until golden and just cooked through, about 5 minutes each side. Transfer to a plate, cover with aluminum foil, and let stand for 10 minutes.

3. Combine the mayonnaise, yogurt, and remaining lime juice in a bowl. Whisk until combined.

4. Slice the chicken. Arrange the lettuce, cucumber, and chicken on serving plates. Drizzle with the dressing and serve.

# CHICKEN & SUGARSNAP salad

Serves 4-6 • Preparation 15 minutes • Cooking 2 minutes
Difficulty 1

| | | | |
|---|---|---|---|
| 12 | ounces (350 g) sugar snap peas, trimmed | 4 | cooked, smoked boneless chicken breasts, thinly sliced |
| 3 | cups (150 g) baby spinach leaves | 1/3 | cup (90 ml) coconut milk |
| 16 | fresh mint leaves | | |

1. Cook the sugar snap peas in boiling water for 2 minutes. Drain and rinse under ice-cold water to stop the cooking process.

2. Combine the sugar snap peas, spinach, and mint in a large bowl. Toss well.

3. Divide the salad among four to six serving plates. Top with the chicken and drizzle with the coconut milk. Serve at room temperature.

# DUCK SALAD with thyme & honey

2    duck breasts, skin on

Salt and freshly ground black pepper

1    tablespoon peanut oil

1    teaspoon butter

1    sprig thyme, leaves picked from the stalk

2    tablespoons honey

1    tablespoon freshly squeezed lemon juice

2    tablespoons walnut oil

2    cups (100 g) mixed salad greens

12    cherry tomatoes, halved

Serves 4 • Preparation 10 minutes • Cooking 15–20 minutes • Difficulty 2

1. Preheat the oven to 375° F (190°C/gas 5). Season the duck breasts with salt and pepper. Heat the peanut oil in a Dutch oven over high heat. Add the duck breasts, skin-side down, and cook until the skin is deep caramel brown.

2. Transfer the Dutch oven to the oven and roast the duck until cooked to your liking; medium-rare will take about 10 minutes. Discard the excess fat and put the duck in a bowl.

3. Heat the butter in a large frying pan over medium heat until it bubbles. Add the thyme and honey. Add the duck, skin-side up, and sauté until well coated, 2–3 minutes. Set aside.

4. Drain the cooking juices into a small bowl. Add the lemon juice, walnut oil, salt, and pepper and whisk together.

5. Divide the salad and tomatoes among four serving plates. Slice the duck breast and place on the salads. Drizzle with the sauce and serve.

# WARM ORIENTAL CHICKEN salad

2 boneless skinless chicken breasts, thinly sliced

4 tablespoons (60 ml) clear honey

2 tablespoons rice vinegar

2 tablespoons soy sauce

1 tablespoon sesame oil

1 clove garlic, crushed

1 (1-inch/2.5 cm) piece fresh ginger, peeled and grated

2 tablespoons sesame seeds, toasted

3 tablespoons coarsely chopped fresh cilantro (coriander)

1 large carrot, julienned

4 scallions (spring onions), shredded

1 cucumber, peeled, halved, seeded, and julienned

1 Chinese (or ordinary) lettuce, finely shredded

Serves 4 • Preparation 15 minutes + 30 minutes to marinate • Cooking 5–10 minutes • Difficulty 1

1. Put the chicken in a bowl. Mix the honey, vinegar, and soy sauce in a small bowl then drizzle over the chicken. Let marinate for about 30 minutes.

2. Heat the sesame oil in a large frying pan over high heat. Add the chicken and marinade and sauté until the chicken is cooked through, 5–10 minutes.

3. Put the cilantro, carrot, scallions, cucumber, and lettuce in a large salad bowl. Add the chicken and its cooking juices. Toss well and serve warm.

# CHICKEN, BEAN & ARUGULA salad

$^1/_3$   cup (90 ml) freshly squeezed lemon juice

3   cloves garlic, finely chopped

2   tablespoons finely chopped fresh basil

1   tablespoon brown sugar

$^1/_2$   cup (125 ml) extra-virgin olive oil

Salt and freshly ground black pepper

2   boneless skinless chicken breasts, sliced

1   (14-ounce/400-g) can white kidney or cannellini beans, drained

2   cups (100 g) baby arugula (rocket) leaves

Fresh cilantro (coriander) leaves

Serves 4 • Preparation 15 minutes • Cooking 10–15 minutes • Difficulty 1

1. Heat a grill pan or griddle over high heat. Whisk the lemon juice, garlic, basil, sugar, and oil in a small bowl. Season with salt and pepper.

2. Grill the chicken until cooked through, 5–7 minutes on each side. During cooking, turn the chicken and baste with two-thirds of the lemon and oil mixture.

3. Mix the beans, arugula, cilantro, and remaining lemon and oil mixture in a bowl. Add the chicken and toss gently. Serve warm.

If you liked this recipe, you will love these as well.

**CHICKEN & CORN**
salad

**WARM CHICKEN**
salad

**DUCK SALAD**
with thyme & honey

# THAI BEEF salad

3 tablespoons freshly squeezed lime juice

2 tablespoons Thai fish sauce

1 tablespoon palm sugar or brown sugar

2 teaspoons Thai red curry paste

1 clove garlic, finely chopped

2 tablespoons + 2 teaspoons peanut oil

1 pound (500 g) rump, fillet, or sirloin steak

3 cups (150 g) curly endive

1 cucumber, thinly sliced lengthwise

20 cherry tomatoes, halved

2 large red chiles, seeded and thinly sliced

¹/₃ cup (15 g) fresh mint leaves

¹/₃ cup (15 g) fresh cilantro (coriander) leaves

¹/₃ cup (15 g) fresh basil leaves

1¹/₂ cups (75 g) mung bean sprouts

¹/₄ cup (40 g) roasted peanuts, coarsely chopped

Serves 4–6 • Preparation 20 minutes + 2 hours to marinate • Cooking 4–6 minutes • Difficulty 1

1. Combine the lime juice, fish sauce, palm sugar, curry paste, garlic, and 2 teaspoons of peanut oil in a medium bowl. Add the beef and toss to coat. Cover with plastic wrap (cling film) and marinate in the refrigerator for 2 hours.

2. Preheat a large, heavy-based frying pan on high heat.

3. Brush the pan with the remaining 2 tablespoons of peanut oil. Remove the beef from the marinade and cook until well browned but rare on the inside, 2–3 minutes each side. Set aside for 5 minutes to rest.

4. Combine the endive, cucumber, tomatoes, chiles, mint, cilantro, and basil in a large bowl. Thinly slice the beef across the grain and add to the salad. Drizzle with the marinade and toss. Top with the bean sprouts and peanuts and serve.

# CHICKEN & FRUIT salad

4 cups (500 g) cooked chicken, cubed (leftover roast chicken or 2 grilled or poached chicken breasts)

4 stalks celery, sliced

1 cup (150 g) **seedless** red or green grapes, sliced

2 fresh peaches, peeled and cubed

½ cup (125 ml) mayonnaise

½ cup (125 ml) sour cream

Salt and freshly ground black pepper

Sprigs of flat-leaf parsley, to garnish

Serves 4 • Preparation 10 minutes + 30 minutes to chill • Difficulty 1

1. Combine the chicken, celery, grapes, and peaches in a large bowl and toss gently.

2. Mix the mayonnaise and sour cream in a small bowl and pour over the salad. Season with salt and pepper.

3. Chill in the refrigerator for 30 minutes. Garnish with the parsley and serve.

*This meaty salad makes a high energy, low-carb lunch. Use chicken or turkey breasts instead of the steak if preferred.*

# STEAK & VEGGIE salad

**Dressing**

| | |
|---|---|
| $1/2$ | cup (125 ml) extra-virgin olive oil |
| 2 | tablespoons balsamic vinegar |
| 2 | cloves garlic, finely chopped |
| $1/4$ | teaspoon crumbled dried chiles or red pepper flakes |
| | Salt and freshly ground black pepper |

**Salad**

| | |
|---|---|
| 1 | pound (500 g) boneless beef sirloin or Porterhouse steak |
| | Salt and freshly ground black pepper |
| 1 | red bell pepper (capsicum), sliced |
| 1 | cup (150 g) sliced mushrooms |
| 6 | cups (300 g) mixed salad greens |

Serves 4 • Preparation 20 minutes + 10 minutes to stand • Cooking 15–20 minutes • Difficulty 1

## Dressing

1. Whisk the oil, balsamic vinegar, garlic, chiles, salt, and pepper in a small bowl.

## Salad

1. Heat a grill pan or barbecue on medium-high heat. Season the beef with salt and pepper.

2. Grill the beef, turning once, until cooked to your liking, 10–15 minutes.

3. Toss the bell pepper and mushrooms with 2 tablespoons of the dressing. Grill until the bell pepper and mushrooms are just tender, about 5 minutes.

4. Let the beef stand for 10 minutes, then slice across the grain. Toss with $1/4$ cup (60 ml) of dressing. Put the salad greens, grilled vegetables, and beef in large bowl and toss to coat. Drizzle with the remaining dressing and serve.

If you liked this recipe, you will love these as well.

**WARM PORK**
salad

**WARM BACON SALAD**
with asparagus & spinach

**BBQ PORK SALAD**
with fresh fruit

# ROAST BEEF salad

Serves 4 • Preparation 10 minutes • Cooking 5 minutes
Difficulty 1

| | | | |
|---|---|---|---|
| 2 | red onions, thickly sliced | 1 | tablespoon white wine vinegar |
| 6 | tablespoons (90 ml) extra-virgin olive oil | 1 | bunch arugula (rocket) |
| | Salt and freshly ground black pepper | 12 | thin slices rare roast beef |
| 1 | tablespoon whole-grain mustard | | |

1. Place a grill pan over medium-high heat. Brush the onions with 1 tablespoon of oil and season with salt and pepper. Grill the onions until just tender, about 2 minutes on each side.

2. Whisk the remaining oil, mustard, and white wine vinegar in a small bowl. Season with salt and pepper.

3. Arrange the arugula on individual serving plates. Top with the roast beef and onions. Drizzle with the mustard dressing and serve with sourdough bread.

# CHICKEN & PINEAPPLE salad

Serves 4-6 • Preparation 15 minutes + 30 minutes to chill
Difficulty 1

| | | | |
|---|---|---|---|
| 4 | cups (500 g) cooked chicken, cubed (leftover roast chicken or 2 grilled or poached chicken breasts) | | Salt and freshly ground black pepper |
| | | 4 | cups (200 g) mixed fresh salad greens |
| 4 | stalks celery, sliced | 2 | hard-boiled eggs, quartered |
| 1 | small fresh pineapple, peeled and chopped | | Fresh cilantro (coriander) leaves, to garnish |
| ½ | cup (125 ml) mayonnaise | | |

1. Combine the chicken, celery, pineapple, and mayonnaise in a bowl. Season with salt and pepper and toss gently. Chill in the refrigerator for 30 minutes.

2. Divide the salad greens evenly among four salad bowls and top with the chicken mixture. Garnish with the egg and cilantro and serve.

# WARM PORK salad

Serves 4-6 • Preparation 15 minutes • Cooking 7-10 minutes
Difficulty 1

| | | | |
|---|---|---|---|
| 2 | cups (100 g) baby spinach leaves | ¼ | teaspoon ground cumin |
| 4 | scallions (spring onions), sliced | | Salt and freshly ground white pepper |
| 16 | cherry tomatoes, sliced | 1 | pound (500 g) pork tenderloin, cut in cubes |
| 1 | cup (150 g) canned corn (sweet corn), drained | 2 | tablespoons extra-virgin olive oil |
| 2 | teaspoons chile powder | ½ | cup (125 ml) freshly squeezed orange juice |
| 1 | clove garlic, finely chopped | 2 | tablespoons freshly squeezed lemon juice |

1. Combine the spinach, scallions, cherry tomatoes, and corn in a salad bowl and set aside.

2. Combine the chile powder, garlic, and cumin in a medium bowl. Add the pork and toss with the spice mixture.

3. Heat the oil in large frying pan over medium high heat. Add the pork and sauté until cooked through, 7-10 minutes. Add the orange and lemon juice and bring to a simmer.

4. Spoon the pork mixture over the salad. Toss and serve.

# LAMB & TOMATO salad

Serves 4-6 • Preparation 15 minutes • Cooking 2 minutes
Difficulty 1

| | | | |
|---|---|---|---|
| 1 | pound (500 g) boneless lamb steaks or lamb tenderloin | 1 | cup (50 g) coarsely chopped flat-leaf parsley |
| 6 | tablespoons (90 ml) extra-virgin olive oil | 8 | ounces (250 g) yellow tomatoes, halved |
| | Salt and freshly ground black pepper | 1 | cucumber, diced |
| 4 | scallions (spring onions), thinly sliced on the diagonal | 2 | teaspoons whole-grain mustard |
| | | 1 | tablespoon honey |

1. Heat a large frying pan over medium-high heat. Rub the lamb with 1 tablespoon of oil and season with salt and pepper. Cook the lamb for 8-10 minutes, turning occasionally, until cooked to your liking. Transfer to a plate, cover with aluminum foil, and let rest.

2. Mix the scallions, parsley, tomatoes, and cucumber in a large salad bowl. Whisk the remaining oil, mustard, and honey in a small bowl. Season with salt and pepper.

3. Thinly slice the lamb and add to the salad. Pour the dressing over the salad, toss gently, and serve.

Be sure to choose tender young asparagus for this recipe. If the stalks are quite fat you can cut them in half lengthwise so that they cook more quickly. When asparagus is not available, replace with 14 ounces (400 g) of green beans.

# WARM BACON SALAD
## with asparagus & spinach

| | |
|---|---|
| 5 | tablespoons (75 ml) extra-virgin olive oil |
| 2 | tomatoes, sliced |
| 16 | tender asparagus stalks, tough parts removed |
| 8 | ounces (250 g) bacon, thinly sliced |
| 1 | fennel bulb, cut into thin wedges |
| 4 | cups (200 g) baby spinach leaves |
| 1 | tablespoon brine-cured green peppercorns, rinsed |
| 2 | tablespoons balsamic vinegar |

Serves 4 • Preparation 15 minutes • Cooking 7–12 minutes • Difficulty 1

1. Heat 1 tablespoon of oil in a large frying pan over medium heat. Add the tomatoes and simmer for 1–2 minutes. Arrange the tomatoes in a layer on a large serving dish.

2. Add 4–6 tablespoons of water to the frying pan and cook the asparagus over high heat until just tender, 3–5 minutes. Layer the asparagus over the tomatoes on the serving dish.

3. Add the bacon to the pan and sauté until crisp, and golden brown, 3–5 minutes. Set aside.

4. Arrange the fennel and spinach on top of the asparagus and top with the bacon. Sprinkle with the peppercorns. Drizzle with the remaining 4 tablespoons of oil and balsamic vinegar and serve warm.

If you liked this recipe, you will love these as well.

**SALAMI & APPLE**
salad

**SMOKED HAM SALAD**
with pineapple

**BBQ PORK SALAD**
with fresh fruit

# SALAMI & APPLE salad

¼ cup (60 ml) extra-virgin olive oil

1 tablespoon cider vinegar

½ teaspoon sugar

Salt and freshly ground black pepper

8 ounces (250 g) diced salami

2 green apples, cored and cut into cubes

5–6 pickled cucumbers (gherkins), drained and sliced

3 tablespoons coarsely chopped flatleaf parsley

1 medium sweet red onion, sliced

Serves 4 • Preparation 15 minutes + 15 minutes to chill • Difficulty 1

1. Whisk the oil, vinegar, and sugar in a small bowl. Season with salt and pepper.

2. Put the salami, apples, pickled cucumbers, and parsley in a large salad bowl. Drizzle with the dressing and toss well. Top with the onion rings. Chill in the refrigerator for 15 minutes before serving.

# SMOKED HAM SALAD with pineapple

1    large apple, peeled, cored, and cut into cubes

8    ounces (250 g) sliced smoked ham, cut in small squares

1    small pineapple, peeled, cored, and cut into cubes

5    ounces (150 g) sauerkraut

$\frac{1}{2}$    cup (125 ml) light mayonnaise

3    tablespoons light (single) cream

    Freshly squeezed juice of 1 lemon

2    teaspoons finely chopped fresh rosemary

1    tablespoon finely chopped fresh dill + extra, to garnish

$\frac{1}{8}$    teaspoon sugar

    Salt

Serves 4 • Preparation 10 minutes • Difficulty 1

1. Combine the apple, ham, and pineapple in a large salad bowl. Add the sauerkraut and toss well.

2. Whisk the mayonnaise, cream, and lemon juice in a small bowl. Add the rosemary, dill, and sugar. Season with salt and mix well.

3. Spoon the dressing over the salad and serve.

Pork goes well with many types of fresh ripe fruit. Vary the fruit in this recipe according to what you like or what you have on hand. Sweet fresh pineapple, peaches, and apples are all good choices.

# BBQ PORK SALAD with fresh fruit

## Salad

| | |
|---|---|
| 1 | pound (500 g) pork fillet or tenderloin |
| 1/4 | cup (60 ml) extra-virgin olive oil |
| | Salt and freshly ground black pepper |
| 1 | tablespoon finely chopped fresh rosemary |
| 1 | clove garlic, finely chopped |
| 6 | cups (300 g) mixed salad greens |
| 2 | ripe nectarines, cut into 12-wedges each |
| 1 | grapefruit, segmented |
| 2 | avocados, cut into wedges |

## Honey Dressing

| | |
|---|---|
| 1/2 | cup (125 ml) extra-virgin olive oil |
| 2 | tablespoons balsamic vinegar |
| 1/2 | tablespoon Dijon mustard |
| 2 | tablespoons honey |
| 2 | tablespoons mayonnaise |
| 1/2 | teaspoon chile powder |
| 1/2 | teaspoon salt |
| 1/2 | teaspoon black pepper |

Serves 4 • Preparation 20 minutes + 12 hours to chill • Cooking 10–15 minutes • Difficulty 2

## Salad

1. Place the pork in a medium bowl. Mix the oil, salt, pepper, rosemary, and garlic in a small bowl and pour over the pork. Turn to coat. Chill in the refrigerator for 12 hours.

2. Preheat a barbecue or grill pan over medium-high heat. Grill until tender and cooked through, 12–15 minutes. Let rest for 10 minutes, then slice thickly.

3. Combine the salad greens, nectarines, grapefruit, and avocadoes in a large salad bowl or divide them among four individual bowls. Top with the pork.

## Honey Dressing

1. Whisk the oil, balsamic vinegar, mustard, honey, mayonnaise, chile powder, salt, and pepper.

2. Drizzle the dressing over the salad and serve.

If you liked this recipe, you will love these as well.

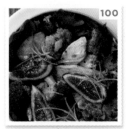

**CHICKEN SALAD**
with figs & broccoli

**CHICKEN & FRUIT**
salad

**SMOKED HAM SALAD**
with pineapple

# INDEX